£4.95

AFTER THE DIVO

Costantino Ledda is convicted fo⸱⸱ ⸱⸱ ⸱⸱⸱
he is innocent. He revolt⸱ ⸱⸱⸱ ⸱⸱⸱ ⸱⸱⸱
clemency are intended to ⸱⸱⸱ ⸱⸱⸱ ⸱n
part, he accepts the verd⸱ ⸱⸱⸱ ⸱e and
murky crime which he h⸱ ⸱⸱⸱ which the
complicity and unheeding s⸱ ⸱⸱ill drive him to
committing. He inhabits a w⸱ ⸱ed by a sinister and
ancient fate which closes inexo⸱ ⸱, upon him. Giovanna Era,
his wife, is impelled by forces beyond her control to betray
both herself and her husband – her inability to decide, let alone
act upon, her own will leads to inevitable destruction.

None of these characters can escape this process, for here
everyone is, at different times, both victim and executioner.
Set in the wild Sardinian countryside, the bitter and ineluctable
drama of *After the Divorce* assumes hallucinatory dimensions:
a secret nocturnal landscape in which men and women
stumble over their own unrecognizable passions.

GRAZIA DELEDDA

Grazia Deledda was born in 1871 in Nuoro, Sardinia where she
lived and wrote until marrying. After her marriage in 1900, she
moved to Rome, but her short stories and novels, written at
first for magazines, continued to treat the wild landscape of her
native Sardinia. In earlier writings romantic descriptions
dominated, but these gradually gave way to a more intense
study of her taciturn characters struggling with a peculiar
form of fatalism against their primitive background (e.g.
Tesoro, 1897; *Elias Portolu*, 1903; *Marianna Sirca*, 1915). This
lyrical treatment of man and nature is well expressed in her
best works: *Cenere* (1904), *L'edera* (1908), *La madre* (1920) and
Naufraghi in porto (1920). After 1921 she abandoned the
Sardinian background, but in essence her art remained the
same (e.g. *Il segreto dell'uomo solitario*, 1921). She was awarded
the Nobel Prize for Literature in 1926. She died in 1936, and her
autobiographical *Cosima* appeared posthumously in 1937.

GRAZIA DELEDDA

After the Divorce

Translated from the Italian by
SUSAN ASHE
With an Introduction by
SHEILA MACLEOD

ENCOUNTER

Quartet Books   London Melbourne New York

First published by Quartet Books Limited 1985
A member of the Namara Group
27/29 Goodge Street, London W1P 1FD

Copyright © 1979 by Arnoldo Mondadori Editore SpA, Milan

Translation copyright © 1985 by Susan Ashe
Introduction copyright © 1985 by Sheila MacLeod

British Library Cataloguing in Publication Data

Deledda, Grazia
After the divorce. — (Quartet encounter)
I. Title   II. Naufraghi in porto. *English*
853'.912[F]   PQ4811.E6
ISBN 0-7043-3485-2

Typeset by AKM Associates (UK) Ltd, Southall, Greater London
Printed and bound in Great Britain
by Whitstable Litho Ltd, Whitstable, Kent

INTRODUCTION

'I am not yet twenty,' Grazia Deledda wrote in 1890; 'by the age of thirty I want to have created a body of work wholly and exclusively Sardinian.' No mean ambition for a girl born in 1871 in what was then one of the most primitive parts of Europe, a girl whose formal education ended when she was eleven years old, and who started to learn Italian only a year later. And yet Grazia Deledda started writing at the age of thirteen, was first published at seventeen and, some forty-five books later, was awarded the Nobel Prize for Literature in 1926.

The roots of her extraordinary ambition and industry remain mysterious, but there is no doubt that her inspiration (she makes one believe afresh in that overworked word) was Sardinia itself. Or, more particularly, it was the remote and mountainous region of the Barbagia around Nuoro to the north of the island. This was (and to a large extent still is) an area beyond or in conflict with the law, an area of banditry, kidnappings and long-running vendettas. D.H. Lawrence, who was one of Deledda's admirers, described it in 1928 as a place

> of rigid conventions, the rigid conventions of barbarism, and at the same time the fierce violence of the instinctive passions. A savage tradition of chastity, with a savage lust of the flesh. A barbaric overlordship of the gentry, with a fierce indomitableness of the servile classes. A lack of public opinion, a lack of belonging to any other part of the world, which makes inland Sardinia almost as savage as Benin . . .

But it is also a landscape of wild and wonderful beauty, a backdrop more suitable to *Wuthering Heights* than to the sentiments of mainstream Italian literature.

After the Divorce is Grazia Deledda's eighth novel, first published in 1902 and subsequently appearing in 1920 with a different title. It is set around the turn of the century. The cruel and miserly Basile Ledda has been murdered and his nephew Costantino arrested, tried, then sent across the sea to prison for twenty-seven years. His young and pretty wife, Giovanna, is left to cope as best she can for their baby son and her ageing mother Bachisia. The future looks bleak and beggarly for the two women, poorest of peasants as they are, without a man to support them and with few opportunities for work of their own in a land devoid alike of rich soil and rich employers. But a new divorce law is about to come into operation, a law which allows for the wives of convicts to divorce their husbands and so, perhaps, remarry. Is there, then, some hope, some way out, for Giovanna and her son? And should there be? This is the moral dilemma of *After the Divorce*, and the consequences of Giovanna's decision to divorce carry the novel through to a conclusion as inevitable as that of any Greek tragedy.

At first the action alternates between Giovanna's village of Orlei and the mainland prison in which Costantino has been wrongfully incarcerated. We see Giovanna missing Costantino, ground down by deprivation, and worn down by her mother's urging her to marry her former suitor, Brontu, the shepherd son of a rich but mean neighbouring widow, Martina Dejas. We see Costantino desperately missing his wife and son and bewildered by the harsh new world of strangers and immediately arbitrary authority. He composes a hymn on behalf of all convicts to his namesake, San Costantino, the patron saint of Orlei, a hymn which he has to write with his own blood and have smuggled out of prison. Neither he nor Giovanna curses God or their fate: scarcely do they even ask why this terrible thing has happened to them. Much less are they motivated towards finding the real murderer, the possibility of whose existence is only glancingly considered. They cannot believe in their own innocence because they do not believe in themselves as people possessing universally recognizable human rights. And yet they are innocent.

In the absence of what Lawrence defines as public opinion, their only moral referents are those of the village community or

tribe; the Church with its pale priesthood which has never quite
been able to conquer the local pre-Christian rituals and beliefs;
and the Law, which is laid down and administered by foreigners
on the other side of the sea. Sometimes those forces mesh into
something approaching a coherent whole, but more often they
are in conflict, and most of the characters are capable of invoking
any one of the three to suit themselves – or in sheer desperation.
Lawrence found 'the human instinct still uncontaminated' in
Deledda's work, but it seems to me that her characters are forever
seeking to justify their instinctive passions in the name of one
authority or another. 'Unevolved' (Lawrence's word again) they
may be in all sorts of ways, but they are in a state of evolution:
the human consciousness struggling towards conscience in an
environment which often seems fitter for conscienceless beasts.

Both Giovanna and Costantino believe that they are being
punished for having contracted a civil marriage rather than
having waited until such time as they could have afforded the
more expensive church ceremony. Their marriage was in accor-
dance with Law, if not with the Church. And so the Church is
prepared to condone the divorce and Giovanna's subsequent
remarriage to Brontu. But Giovanna's decision is by no means
wholly that of a devout Catholic: her son has died of malnutrition
and, according to the mores of the tribe which places a high value
on paternity and its proof, there need now be no shame accruing
to Brontu in the raising of another man's child. Similarly, the
child will not have to undergo the ignominy of knowing his
mother, as she is known to her neighbours, as 'the woman with
two husbands'. When the child of the new union is born 'green
and sickly' and fails to thrive, no one is surprised: after all, his
parents are living in mortal sin. But they have also contravened
the mores of the tribe: if Giovanna and Brontu had simply lived
together, no one would have blamed them overly: the flesh is
weak, life is hard, and saintly beggarliness not natural to the
young and attractive. It is the fact that they have invoked the
higher authorities of the Law and (to a lesser extent) the Church
to justify their behaviour which arouses moral indignation.

In flouting the unwritten mores of the tribe, Giovanna and
Brontu have, as it were, brought unconscious material (the
manner in which ordinary people live their unsanctioned but all

too human lives) into consciousness. Because both Law and Church have recognized and condoned their conduct, it can no longer be regarded as part of the submerged behaviour of the tribe, the sort of behaviour by which it has managed to preserve its independence of either authority. Thus the cohesiveness of the tribe itself is threatened. Its members must now attempt some form of reconciliation among the three conflicting loyalties.

Some condemn the Law which can allow remarriage without widowhood, rejecting it as the immune system rejects a foreign body. According to this view, the Church has to pay lip-service to the Law, but has shown its disapproval in Father Elias's refusal to attend the new baby's baptismal feast. Others condemn the Church, castigating Father Elias and his colleagues as vacillating and cowardly. Their confidence, which was never particularly strong in the first place (apart from personal allegiances to San Costantino and the Virgin) has now been shattered. When one of the villagers is bitten by a tarantula, the neighbours enact a pagan rite to cure him, and a procession of seven widows, seven married women and seven virgins, dances and sings its mournful way through the streets. Order – the fragile order which depends on the tension among split allegiances – has been disrupted.

There are many who can condemn both Giovanna and Brontu as individuals, citing lust and greed, but there are few prepared to condemn the tribe – and those only in part. One such is the fisherman and leech-gatherer, Isidoro Pane, who alone of the congregation actually listens to Father Elias's sermons and can find compassion in his heart for the wretched Giovanna and Costantino as well as the yet more wretched real murderer. Curiously enough, Isidoro is a figure reminiscent of Words-worth's leech-gatherer, a lonely self-sufficient man, a bit of an outcast, and a character in whom the reader is expected to find some unspecified embodiment of wisdom. Like others of Deledda's characters he could well belong in the *Lyrical Ballads* beside Simon Lee or the Mad Mother: all have the same understated but monumental quality of standing stones whose endurance speaks of a mysterious 'resolution and independence' beyond the exigencies of circumstance.

But Grazia Deledda is as far from drawing Wordsworth's moral conclusions (although I suspect she may share some of them) as she is from making a virtue out of simplicity. Indeed she is one of the least sentimental writers I have ever come across and knows all too well that simplicity is a necessity which, on rare occasions, can be converted to a virtue but is more likely to be synonymous with ignorance and hence perhaps meanness, jealousy, greed and spite. The characters in *After the Divorce* are not divided into good and bad, or even into sympathetic and unsympathetic. Each has his/her moments of strength and weakness, doubt and faith, purity and corruption. It is the shared circumstance of deprivation which arouses sympathy, and the surging, faltering struggle towards a greater humanity which engages and compels.

To judge by the translation, Grazia Deledda is no great stylist and her prose, though capable of lyricism, is without tricks or flourishes. Italian critics have found it difficult to 'place' her in their own literature, and one (Paolo Milano in a 1982 Radio Three programme, 'The Cactus and the Rope') has gone so far as to claim that she was awarded the Nobel 'because she was so Scandinavian'. Far-fetched though this may seem, I think there may be a grain of truth in the claim. There is something Northern and Protestant rather than Southern and Catholic in Deledda's perceptions, thought and overall thrust. Although the milieu she describes is very different from that of Ibsen or Strindberg, there is, as Paolo Milano hints, a similar emphasis on guilt and the possibility (which is often to say, the impossibility) of absolution. I myself was often reminded of the Walter Scott couplet:

> O Caledonia stern and wild,
> Meet nurse for a poetic child.

As often with Scandinavian or Scottish writers, Deledda's Sardinian landscape and her unadorned prose are all of a piece: the sparseness and the apparent harshness have a beauty of their own which often verges on the poetic.

And yet ... I find that Paolo Milani's comments, perceptive as they are, also fail to 'place' Grazia Deledda. It seems to me that there is no absolution in *After the Divorce* because there was never any real guilt. It is not the Protestant we are dealing with but the Pagan. If the outcome of the novel seems pessimistic, it is not because human sin lacks divine redemption but because human existence at its most existential and threadbare gives little cause for optimism. Any struggle towards self-awareness, whether individual or collective, must be a poignant one, and yet it is in the struggle itself that the cause for optimism lies. The individual may be defeated by circumstances – the Law, the Church, the tribe or, even more surely, poverty – but the fact that she/he has seen fit to fight and question, however misplaced the target, is in itself a sign of victory.

If this were not so, Grazia Deledda's writing would be unrelievedly gloomy, unreadable. But *After the Divorce*, although sombre indeed at times, is not a depressing novel and seems not to have been written out of despair. On the contrary, it shines and sometimes burns with love and compassion for Sardinia and its people, a love and compassion which never amount to conflagration but maintain a pure and steady flame.

Sheila MacLeod

After the Divorce

I

On the floor by the bed in the Porrus' guest room a woman wept. She crouched, rocking her head on her arms, sobbing in utter despair. Her shapely figure, tightly laced into a yellow cotton bodice, rose and sank like a wave on the sea.

It was almost dark in the windowless room. Through the open door, which gave on to a bricked balcony, could be seen a stretch of ash-grey sky that was gradually darkening. In it, a single yellow star shone. From the courtyard below a cricket chirped, and now and then a horse's hoof stamped against the cobbles.

A stout old woman in the peasant dress of Nuoro appeared in the doorway carrying an iron lamp in one of whose four sockets burned a wick swimming in oil. 'Giovanna Era, what are you doing there in the dark?' she called out in a loud, gruff voice. 'It sounds to me as if you're crying.'

The sobbing went on. The old woman drew closer and went on indignantly. 'There's your mother downstairs waiting for you, and here you are wailing like a madwoman.' Hooking the lamp to a nail in the wall, she crossed to the weeping girl, trying to find words of comfort. But all she could say was, 'You're crazy, Giovanna.'

The guest room, traditionally reserved for friends from neighbouring villages, was large, whitewashed, and unplastered, and it contained a big wooden bedstead and a table covered with a fine cotton cloth. On the table were little glass cups and saucers. A number of pictures adorned the walls close under the rough wooden ceiling. Bunches of wrinkled grapes and yellow pears hung from the rafters, filling the room with a delicate fragrance. Sacks stuffed with wool stood about the floor.

The old woman, who was mistress of the house, took hold of one of these sacks, dragged it to the centre of the room, then back again to where she had found it. 'Just stop that at once,' she said, panting from her effort. 'You mustn't give up yet. Even if the prosecutor asks for hard labour, it doesn't mean the jury will follow him like a pack of mad dogs.'

Still the desperate sobbing continued.

'Get up or I'll call your mother,' snarled the woman, seizing the girl and forcing her head up.

The girl had a lovely face, round and rosy and ringed by a tangle of black hair. From beneath thick brows her tear-stained dark eyes glistened. 'Leave me alone to my fate, Porredda,' she screamed. 'Thirty years. That's what they'll give him!'

'Fate or no fate, get up. Anyway, what's thirty years? You're carrying on like a wildcat.'

In a frenzy, Giovanna cried out and tore her hair. 'What's thirty years? A man's whole life, Porredda. You don't understand a thing. Go away and leave me alone, for the love of God.'

'Get up, damn you, and stop all this,' Porredda said. 'There'll be plenty of time to tear your hair out tomorrow. Your husband hasn't been sentenced yet.'

Giovanna dropped her head and began to cry again, heartbroken. 'Costantino, Costantino,' she wailed. 'I'll never see you again, never again. Those mad dogs have taken you and shackled you, and they'll never let you go. Our house will be empty, our bed cold, our family broken up.'

Giovanna's grief moved Porredda. Not knowing what else to do, the old woman went out on to the balcony and called. 'Bachisia, come up here. Your daughter's losing her mind.'

There was a footstep on the outer staircase. Porredda came in again, followed by a tall, tragic-looking woman dressed in black. Her yellow, hawklike face and gleaming green eyes were framed by a black scarf. Her mere presence seemed to have a calming effect on the girl.

'Get up!' the tall woman said in a harsh voice.

Giovanna rose. She was a tall girl, well-built yet slim. Her short woollen skirt had a purple stripe that swelled over muscular thighs and a green hem that revealed small feet and two shapely legs.

'Why are you being so troublesome?' her mother said. 'Stop it at once and come down to dinner. Don't frighten the children or spoil these good people's happiness.'

'These good people's happiness' referred to the arrival that same evening of the son of the house, a law student home for the holidays.

Giovanna obeyed, calming herself. She took the woollen kerchief off her head, uncovering a cap of old brocade, from which tumbled torrents of jet black hair, and went to wash in a basin of water placed on a chair. Porredda looked at Bachisia, pressed her finger to her lips, and left without a sound.

Bachisia said nothing. She waited until Giovanna had bathed her face and tidied her hair, then both women silently descended the outside stairs. It was a warm, still night. The first small yellow star had been followed by thousands of silver stars, and the Milky Way lay across the sky like a huge veil embroidered with twinkling jewels. A smell of new-mown hay permeated the air. Concealed in the courtyard trellis, crickets still chirped, and the horse munched, stamping its iron-shod hooves. From some way off came the sound of a mournful song.

The kitchen door and that of a ground-floor room occasionally used as a dining-room were wide-open to the courtyard. In the kitchen, beside the kindled hearth, Porredda was busy preparing macaroni. A fair-haired girl, barefoot and dishevelled, squabbled with a boy who was as fat and florid as his grandmother.

'Stop it or I'll thrash you with this ladle, you wicked children,' Porredda said, chasing them off. As they escaped into the courtyard they collided with Giovanna and her mother.

'What is it? What's going on?'

'They drive me to distraction,' said old Porredda from the kitchen door.

Just then the dark figure of a girl moved away from the half-open street door, calling excitedly, 'They're coming, Grandmother! They're here!'

'Let them in, and do your best to look after your brother and sister, Grazia.'

Grazia did not reply, but took the lamp from Bachisia's hand, snuffed it out, and hid it behind a bench in the kitchen. 'Now that Uncle Paolo is here you ought to be ashamed of this lamp, Grandmother.'

'Why? Do you think Paolo was brought up on gold?'

'But he's been to Rome.'

'So what? They have no lamps like this in Rome because there they have to buy their oil by the pennyworth, while here we can use as much oil as we like.'

'You'll be in trouble if you believe that,' said the girl, and she turned back to the courtyard in a flutter at hearing the voices of her uncle and her grandfather.

'Hello, Giovanna . . . Bachisia, how are you?' said the hearty voice of the student. 'I'm well, thank the Lord. I was so sorry to hear about your misfortune. Bear up, who knows what may happen. It's tomorrow they're pronouncing sentence, isn't it?'

He led the way into the room where the table was laid, followed by the women and children, whom their uncle's presence intimidated and delighted at one and the same time. He limped slightly, one foot being smaller and the leg shorter than the other. For this he was nicknamed Dr Pededdu ('Little Foot'), which he did not mind, saying it was better to have one foot smaller than the other than a head smaller than anyone else's. He was short too. His round pink face with its blondish moustache smiled shyly from beneath a floppy soft hat.

Sitting down on the bed with his legs dangling, he pressed his nephew and niece to him, one on each side. They stared at him open-mouthed as he hugged them absent-mindedly, his attention riveted on the tale Bachisia was telling him. From time to time he glanced at Grazia, whose tall, angular, girlish figure was accentuated by a black dress that was too small for her. Her steel-grey eyes were fixed on her uncle in a stubborn, eager gaze.

4

'Well,' said Bachisia in her harsh voice, 'this is what happened. Costantino had an uncle, his father's brother. His name was Basile Ledda, but they called him the Vulture because he was so greedy for money. God rest his soul if he's not already in the devil's clutches. He was a morose man, a sour old miser. They say his wife died of starvation. As a boy, Costantino was put in his charge. The child had some money of his own and the uncle devoured every penny of it, then he beat Costantino, bound him between two rocks in a field, and left him to the mercy of the sun and the bees, which almost stung his eyes out. One day when he was sixteen, Costantino ran away. He was gone for three years. He said he'd been working in the mines, I don't know, but that's what he said.'

'Yes, he was working in the mines,' Giovanna broke in.

'I don't know about that,' said her mother, pursing her lips dubiously. 'Anyway, the fact remains that one day during the time Costantino was away someone took a shot at the Vulture while he was out in the fields. So he must have had enemies. When Costantino came back he admitted that he hated his uncle and had run away to keep from killing him. However, Costantino made his peace with the old man. Now listen to this, Paolo Porru.'

'Dr Porru! Dr Pededdu!' squealed the grandson, correcting the guest. Bachisia looked angrily at the boy and made as if to strike him. Giovanna laughed. Seeing their 'heartbroken guest' who until then had been surrounded by a halo of romance and tragedy laughing, Grazia broke into a nervous giggle too. Then Minnia, the younger sister, giggled and then the boy and the student laughed. Bachisia looked round, glaring. Why were they laughing? She raised a thin yellow hand to slap someone. But whom? Her daughter? The boy? Then Porredda came in with the steaming macaroni.

Behind her came Efes Maria Porru, thickset and imposing, wearing a tight-fitting blue velvet jerkin. Though a peasant, he made himself out to be a well-read man, and his sallow face with its short curly beard and bright eyes showed a certain intelligence.

'Come quickly, supper's ready,' said Porredda, putting the

dish down in the centre of the table. 'I see you are all laughing. Is it the doctor who's making you laugh?'

'I was about to slap your grandson,' said Bachisia.

'Why, my dear? Come and eat now. Giovanna here, Dr Porreddu over there.'

Paolo threw himself back flat on the bed, stretched out his arms, lifted his legs in the air, dropped them again, and jumped down on to his feet yawning. Giovanna and the children burst out laughing again.

'A little gymnastics does you good,' Paolo said. 'God how I'll sleep tonight. All my bones are dislocated. You're so tall, Grazia – you're like a beanpole.'

The girl blushed and lowered her eyes; Bachisia scowled, offended because the student's mind was on something other than her story and because everyone was making light of Costantino's calamity. Even Giovanna seemed to have forgotten, and only when Porredda put in front of her a big helping of macaroni, pink and fragrant with sauce, did the young woman's face go dark again and she refuse to eat.

'What did I tell you?' exclaimed Porredda. 'She's out of her mind. Why don't you eat? What does eating now have to do with the sentence tomorrow?'

'Come on now,' said Bachisia, a bit crossly. 'Don't be foolish. Don't spoil these good people's happiness.'

Efes Maria tied his napkin under his chin, and spat out a literary epigram. 'Dante says, "A brave heart defies fate." Come now, Giovanna. Show us that you're a mountain flower, and you can endure more than the stones themselves. Time heals everything.'

Giovanna began to eat, but with a lump in her throat; Paolo said nothing but was bent over his food so that by the time Giovanna had managed to swallow her first mouthful his plate was already clear.

'You're just like a whirlwind, my son,' said Porredda. 'You're hungry as a wolf. Do you want any more? There's plenty.'

'It looks as if you didn't have much to eat in the Eternal City,' said Efes.

'That's what I say,' agreed Porredda. 'It may be a fine place, but everything there has to be paid for in hard cash. I've heard all about it. They don't keep food in the house the way we do, and when there's no food in the larder you know quite well no one gets enough to eat.'

Bachisia nodded. She knew only too well what a house without food was like.

'Is it true or not, Dr Porreddu?'

'It's true,' he said, eating and laughing and waving his white hands with their over-long nails.

'Maybe that's why he's become such a leech, a vampire,' Efes Maria remarked, turning to his guests. 'He won't leave me a drop of blood in my veins. By God, how they eat up money in Rome!'

'If you only knew,' sighed Paolo. 'Everything is so expensive. A peach costs twenty *centesimi*. There, now I feel better.'

'Twenty *centesimi*!' they all echoed.

'Well, Bachisia? What happened after Costantino came back?' Paolo said.

'As I said, he was away for three years.'

'Yes, he was working in the mines. Then he came back and made peace with his uncle.'

'And then he met my Giovanna here and they fell in love. His uncle was against it because we were poor. So uncle and nephew began hating each other again. Costantino was working for the Vulture and was never paid a penny. Then Costantino came to me and said, "I'm poor. I haven't enough money to buy a wedding-ring or food for guests, and you're poor too, so this is what we'll do. We'll have a civil wedding for the time being. We'll all work. We'll save up enough money to have guests and then Giovanna and I will marry in church." Nowadays lots of people do this, and we decided we would too. The civil wedding took place quietly and afterwards we all lived together. The Vulture went into a rage. He took to shouting and swearing right outside our own front door, and he provoked Costantino everywhere he went. But we kept on working. After the grape harvest last year, while we were baking cakes for the wedding, the uncle was found murdered in his own house. The evening before, Costantino had been

7

seen going in there. He had gone to tell his uncle about the wedding and to try to make peace with him. Poor boy! He didn't try to run away, as I advised him to do.'

'Because he was innocent, heaven help him,' Giovanna broke in.

'There she goes again! If you don't keep quiet I won't go on. Anyway, Costantino was arrested, and now the prosecution is asking for hard labour. They have evidence, to be sure. Costantino was seen going into his uncle's house, where the old man lived alone. That part is true, but there's no proof that Costantino killed him. Costantino seemed full of contradictions and remorse. He kept saying, "It's a mortal sin." He's a devout man, you see, and he believed he was being punished because he and Giovanna lived together without being married in church.'

'Have you any children?' Paolo asked Giovanna.

'Yes, one. Mother of God, what would I do if I didn't have him? If Costantino is found guilty and I didn't have the baby, what would I do?' She seized her hair by the roots and shook her head wildly, half mad with grief.

'The new divorce law is going to be passed soon,' Paolo said. 'A woman whose husband is serving a long sentence can become free again.'

Giovanna seemed not to have understood his words and continued to shake her head from side to side.

'It's wicked. Only God can dissolve a marriage,' Porredda said resolutely.

'Yes, I read about it in the paper,' Efes Maria said rather scornfully. 'They have this divorce now on the mainland. There, men and women get married again and again without priest or mayor. But here – '

'Here too, here too!' said Bachisia, who understood the whole thing.

After supper, Bachisia and Giovanna went to see Costantino's lawyer.

'Where are they sleeping?' asked Paolo. 'The guest room?'

'Of course, why?'

'Because I'd like to sleep there. It's suffocating down here.

What better guest than I?'

'Be patient until tomorrow, my son. They're poor people.'

'Oh God, these barbarous customs, when will they end?' he said irritably.

'I wonder about that too,' said Efes Maria, who had begun reading the newspaper.

'Have you seen the Pope, my son?' asked Porredda to change the subject.

'No.'

'What! You've been in Rome all this time and you haven't been to see the Pope?'

'What do you expect? The Pope is kept inside a box, and you have to pay quite a bit to see him.'

'Oh go on with you!' she said. 'You're an unbeliever.' And she rushed out into the courtyard where the children were fighting like gamecocks, plunged in between them, and pulled them apart. 'My goodness, you're a naughty pair. Oh, you're all wicked, every one of you!'

In the still night, the children's sobs mingled with the chirping of the crickets.

II

The next morning Giovanna was the first to wake. Through a small pane of glass set in the door came the rosy glow of dawn, and the twittering swallows broke the early-morning silence. She remembered that this was the day that would decide her husband's fate. She was sure Costantino would be found guilty, but she went on hoping against hope. As to whether or not he were guilty, she had never given it much thought. It was only the consequence, the thought of being parted perhaps for ever from the man she loved, that tortured her. As the full consciousness of this struck her she felt such anguish that she jumped from the bed and began to dress, saying breathlessly, 'It's late, it's late.'

Bachisia opened her small firefly-like eyes and she too got up. She knew only too well what that day and the day after and a year or two or ten years after would bring to let herself get worked up. She dressed, dipped her hands in the water and passed them across her face once. Then she dried her face and, with great care, arranged the folds of her scarf about her head.

'It's late,' Giovanna kept on. 'Oh God, it's late.'

Her mother's calm quietened the girl. Giovanna followed Bachisia down into the kitchen, where Bachisia prepared coffee and bread for Costantino (they were allowed to take food to the prisoner), put everything into a basket, and the two set off for the prison.

The streets were deserted. The sun rose up from behind Mount Orthobene, and the sky was so blue, the birds so joyous, and the air so still and fragrant, that it was like a holiday morning. Giovanna crossed the street, which led from

10

the station, near where the Porru family lived, to the prison. Looking up at the distant purple mountains that hemmed in the great wild valley, she inhaled the air full of the scent of wild flowers, thought of her little house, of her baby, of her lost happiness – and felt she was dying.

Her mother strode on in front with the basket on her head. They reached the stark white bulk of the prison. In the silent early-morning glow the sentry stood still and mute as a statue. A single green shrub growing against the blank wall accentuated the dreariness of the place. The prison's outer door, which gaped and closed from time to time like the mouth of a sphinx, opened to engulf the two women. Everyone inside the dismal cavern had come to know them, from the florid, solemn chief warder, who looked like a general, down to the pale young guard who, with his straight blond moustache, aped elegance.

The gloomy, smelly passageway gave some idea of the horrors that lay beyond. The two women were allowed no further; the young guard came forward and took the basket, and Giovanna asked him in a low voice if Costantino had slept.

'Yes, he slept, but he kept dreaming and saying the words "mortal sin" over and over again.'

'May he go to the devil with that mortal sin of his,' said Bachisia. 'Why doesn't he stop it?'

'Why are you cursing him? Hasn't fate cursed him enough already?' hissed Giovanna.

Outside again, they waited for the prisoner to be brought forth. When Giovanna saw the *carabinieri* who were to take him to the court, she began to tremble violently. Her black eyes widened as she fixed a half mad look on the great doorway. Anguished moments passed. Once more the sphinx's mouth opened, and surrounded by stony-faced guards with long black moustaches the figure of Costantino appeared. He was tall and lithe as a young poplar. Two locks of black hair, long and shining, framed a beardless, almost effeminate face that had grown pallid from confinement. He had chestnut-brown eyes, an innocent boyish mouth, and a dimpled chin.

The moment he saw Giovanna he went whiter still and

stopped short, resisting the guards. The girl rushed forward, sobbing, and clutched his manacled hands.

'Move along,' said one of the *carabinieri*, then, gently, to her: 'You know that's not allowed, my dear.'

Bachisia had stepped forward as well, her little green eyes darting over the group.

'Be brave,' Costantino said in a firm, almost cheerful voice, and he gave Giovanna a brave smile.

'The lawyer is waiting for you at the court,' said Bachisia as the guards pushed the two women gently aside.

'Stand back, you people,' they said, leading the prisoner off.

Still smiling at Giovanna, his white teeth gleaming between colourless lips, Costantino moved away flanked by his two stony-faced guards.

Bachisia dragged off Giovanna, who was trying to follow her husband, and she led her away to the Porrus' for breakfast before going to the courtroom.

Sunlight flooded the courtyard, playing on the shining leaves of the grapevines from which hung bunches of unripe grapes like pale green marble. The swallows twittered in the sunny air, and Efes Maria, mounted on a bay horse, prepared to set out for the fields. How bright and cheerful seemed that spot with its low stone wall, beyond which stretched a vast horizon. Seated on the kitchen doorstep, the children ate their bread and milk. Grazia had taken hers to eat in a corner, perhaps to avoid the eyes of her student-uncle who, in his shirt-sleeves, stood in the middle of the yard gulping down a huge bowlful of broth.

Porredda polished his shoes, marvelling to hear of the wonderful things he had seen.

'How big is St Peter's? Well, it's as big as a cow byre. You can't even pray there. No one can pray in a cow byre. The angels that hold up the holy water stoup, the smallest ones, are as big as these doors.'

'Then you need a ladder to reach the holy water?'

'No, because they're kneeling, I think. Give me a bit more coffee, Mamma. Is there any?'

'Of course there is. You've come back as hungry

as a shark, my little Paolo.'

'You know what! I've seen dolphins in the sea. Oh, here are our guests. Good morning.'

Telling them of the meeting with her husband, Giovanna was again on the verge of tears, but Porredda took her by the hand and led her into the kitchen.

'You need all your strength today, my dear,' she said, handing the girl a large cup of coffee. 'Drink it up now.'

A little later the two women left for the court, Paolo promising to join them there.

'Courage,' said Porredda. Giovanna could already hear her husband's conviction in her hostess's voice, and she went off with the look of a whipped dog.

Paolo followed her with his eyes, then he said something curious. 'Listen to me. Before two years are out that young woman will be married again.'

'What do you mean, Dr Pededdu?' cried his mother, who always called her son by his nickname when she was angry with him. 'You're crazy.'

'Oh, Mother, I've been across the sea! Let's hope in any case that she'll take me on as her lawyer!'

'That young man wolfs his food,' said Giovanna to her mother as they went down a steep little street. 'May the Lord have mercy on him.'

Bachisia, who was walking along in deep thought, replied between clenched teeth, 'He'll make a good lawyer. He'll gnaw his clients to the bone. Then he'll swallow them whole.'

Silent again, they walked on. A moment later Bachisia stumbled, and as she did so it came to her out of the blue that if one day her daughter were to apply for a divorce, she would ask Paolo to be their lawyer.

When they reached the court-house its windows still reflected the early-morning sun. In the little square some people from Giovanna's village, witnesses at the trial, gathered round the two women, repeating the inevitable commonplace: 'Courage! Courage!'

'Oh yes, we've plenty of that. Now leave us alone,' said Bachisia, striding along, proud as a wild mare. By now the way was familiar, and they went straight to the fateful chambers. Giovanna went in behind her mother, and the others followed, among them a handful of loafers and a lanky, toothless woman with a squint.

The jurors, most of them old and fat, were already in their seats. Some had thick beards and fierce eyes, and they looked as if they had already found the accused guilty. The judge had a good-natured pink face, fringed by a straggly white beard; the prosecutor, with his straight blond moustache and arrogant red face, made no attempt to hide his intent. All the officials – the registrars, the ushers and clerks with their black gowns – looked to Giovanna like cruel sorcerers waiting to cast a mortal spell on poor Costantino.

He stood in the dock like a large trembling bird, between the two stony-faced *carabinieri*, and he looked at Giovanna, but without smiling now. He seemed overwhelmed by dejection and before these arbiters of his fate, his clear childlike eyes grew dark with terror.

Giovanna too felt the grip of an iron hand that squeezed on her heart, and at times the sensation was so sharp as to give her a stab of physical pain.

The lawyer, a small sallow-faced young man, had begun to speak in a high-pitched feminine voice. His defence had been weak. Now he was repeating what he had already said, and his words fell into the void like drops of water into a cave.

The prosecutor maintained an air of indifference. Some of the jurors seemed to think they were performing important work just by sitting there patiently. The others looked as if they were not even listening. Only Bachisia and Giovanna and the prisoner were paying attention to the defence speech, and the longer their lawyer spoke the more they felt that their case was hopelessly lost.

From time to time a new arrival would come in and Giovanna would turn quickly to see if it were Paolo. For some reason she found herself anxiously awaiting him, almost as if his mere presence might help them in some way.

When at last the lawyer finished, Costantino got to his feet, turning red in the face, and asked if he could speak, 'My – my

14

lawyer,' he said, pointing in the man's direction, 'has spoken – has defended me – and I thank him. But he did not say – he did not say – what I wanted him to.' He stopped, breathing hard.

'Add anything to your defence that you feel necessary,' said the judge.

The prisoner stood with his eyes cast down and grew pale again. Then he passed his hand convulsively across his forehead and lifted his head.

'I – ' he began in a low voice. ' I – ' He could go no further. He clenched his fists, turned fiercely to his lawyer and cried out in a strong voice, 'I'm innocent. I tell you I am innocent!'

The lawyer motioned with his hand to quiet him. The judge raised his eyebrows as if to say, 'He may have said it a hundred times, but is it our fault we can't believe him?' A woman's sob rang through the courtroom.

Giovanna had broken down, and Bachisia dragged her, struggling and weeping, towards the door. Everyone except the prosecutor gave the two women a glance of compassion.

Shortly afterwards the court withdrew to deliberate. Followed by two neighbours, Bachisia led Giovanna into the little square, where, instead of comforting her, she scolded her.

'If you don't keep quiet I'll give you a good beating,' she cried.

'Mamma, Mamma,' sobbed the girl. 'They're going to find him guilty. They're going to take him away from me, and there's nothing I can do.'

'What do you expect to do?' one neighbour said. 'Be patient, and let's wait a little longer.'

At that moment three black figures appeared, one of them laughing and limping. It was Paolo Porru with two young priests, friends of his.

'There she is,' said the student. 'It looks as if he's been sentenced already.'

'My word,' observed one of the priests, 'she's as wild and violent as an unbroken filly.'

The other one stared curiously at Giovanna, then all three went up to the women and Paolo asked if the case had been heard. 'It's the man who murdered his uncle?' one of the priests asked.

The other one went on staring at Giovanna, who had begun to regain her self-control.

'He has killed no one!' said Bachisia haughtily. 'You're the murderers, you black crows.'

'If we're crows, you're a witch,' replied the priest. Some of the bystanders laughed.

Giovanna, meanwhile, who on Paolo's solicitation had calmed down, promised not to make a scene if they let her go back into the courtroom. They all went back in together. The jury, after a brief deliberation, were taking their seats again. A profound silence fell upon the dim, hot room. Giovanna heard a fly buzzing at one of the window bars. She felt as if her limbs were growing heavy, as if bars of cold iron were piercing her body and legs and arms.

The judge read out the sentence in a low, indifferent voice, while the prisoner stared holding his breath. Again Giovanna heard the fly buzzing, and a feeling of hatred surged through her, not so much because of what the judge was saying but because he said it with such an air of indifference. That voice was delivering a twenty-seven-year prison sentence upon 'the murderer who, after long premeditation, had committed the crime against the person of his guardian, his own uncle.'

Giovanna had so prepared herself to expect thirty years that for an instant twenty-seven seemed considerably less. But at once she realized that three years in thirty meant nothing, and she had to bite her lips so as not to cry out. Her eyes clouded over. With a desperate effort of will she forced herself to look at Costantino and saw, or seemed to see, his face grey and aged, and his eyes misted and confused. He did not look at her. He never gave her another glance. He was already cut off from her for ever. He was dead, while still among the living. They had killed him, those fat, self-satisfied men who sat there coolly awaiting their next victim. She felt her reason cloud over. Suddenly a wild cry echoed through the room. Someone took hold of her and dragged her out into the sunlit square.

'What do you think you're doing? Are you mad? You were howling like a wild beast,' said Bachisia, clutching her daughter by the arm. 'What good is that? There's still the Court of Appeal, so for the love of God be quiet now.'

The witnesses, the lawyer, and Paolo Porru crowded round the two women and tried to console them. Giovanna wept tearlessly, sobbing in a heartbroken way. Disjointed words and phrases, expressions of tenderness for Costantino, threats for the jurors burst from her trembling lips. She begged them at least to let her see the condemned man led away, and when he appeared between two cold, impassive *carabinieri* – pale, bent, sunken-eyed, prematurely aged – she rushed forward. As the guards did not stop, she began to walk backwards, smiling at Costantino, telling him the Court of Appeal would put everything right and that she would sell her last rag to save him. He gaped at her, his eyes full of shock, while the *carabinieri* pushed him along and one of them said, 'Go away, woman. Go away now and be patient.'

'Go away, Giovanna,' Costantino said too. 'Try to get permission to see me before I'm taken away. Bring the child and be brave.'

She went back with her mother to their hosts' house, where Porredda embraced the two women and burst into tears. Then, furious at herself for breaking down, she set about to make amends, saying, 'Well, what are twenty-seven years? Suppose he'd been sentenced to thirty, wouldn't that have been worse? You don't want to go home now? Not in this heat? You must be crazy, both of you. I won't let you go.'

'No,' said Bachisia. 'We'll go, because the others are going back too and they'll be company for us. But if it won't put you out too much Giovanna will return in a few days with the baby.'

'Bless you. Our house is yours.'

They sat down at the table. Giovanna, though perfectly calm, did not eat. Once or twice Porredda tried to talk on some neutral subject. She asked if the baby had got its first teeth yet, she observed that perhaps it would be bad for him to travel in the heat, then she asked if there had been a good barley crop in the Eras' home village.

As soon as they had finished eating, the two women saddled their horse, packed their saddlebags, and said goodbye. Paolo promised to see their lawyer about the appeal, and as soon as they were out of sight he began playing with his niece, pretending to be mad. He laughed wildly, shaking all over. Suddenly he stopped, grew sad, his eyes staring, then he burst out laughing again.

The girls too began to laugh madly, and the sun-baked courtyard and the whole peaceful house, freed from the tragic presence of the grieving guests, echoed with merriment in the peace of the afternoon.

III

The women rode beneath the hot July sun. They had to go down into the valley and along the bottom and then up again to scale the purple mountains that barred the horizon, where the wild peaks vanished in the ashen glow of the summer haze. It was a melancholy journey. The two women were mounted together on one docile, dejected-looking horse. Their travelling companions made their way in straggling groups, some in front of them and some behind, oppressed by the heat, the stillness and their pained feelings. They grieved for Costantino almost as keenly as the women themselves, and out of respect for Giovanna's dumb misery they either kept silent or, if they did venture to speak, did so in undertones that failed to break the vast silence of the hour and of the countryside.

On and on they went. The valley dropped down to a dry river bed where the road, though not steep, was rugged and at times hard to follow as it wound up barren slopes, between rocky outcrops, dusty scrub, and yellow stubble. Strange trees, wild and solitary as hermits, rose up at long intervals, dumb and lifeless against a background of desolate brightness. Their shadow fell across the ground like the shadow of a lone cloud, confused, terrified by the vast expanse of light broken by its presence alone. Sometimes the shrill cry of a bird rose from this shadow, only to die away, defeated by the silence it had interrupted.

Big purple thistles, pink-belled bindweed, and lilac mallows, challenging the sun, increased the valley's desolation. Endless low stone walls covered with dry yellowed moss, scorched by the sun, meandered up and down. Unripe fields of wheat, whose yellow ears looked like a mass of thorns, ringed in the silent horizon.

As she rode on and on, Giovanna felt her head burning under her woollen kerchief, and silent tears rolled down her face. Seated on the horse's crupper, she tried to hide her tears from her mother, who sat astride the saddle. But Bachisia seemed to see even out of the back of her head and at last she could hold back no longer.

'Listen, my dear,' she said suddenly as they crossed the floor of the valley, 'can't you be good enough to stop that? Why must you go on crying? Haven't you known it for months and months?'

Instead of stopping, however, Giovanna sobbed aloud.

'Can you really be so stupid?' Bachisia said bitterly, giving vent to her feelings. 'Did he or didn't he kill the Vulture? Of course he killed him.'

'He never said he did.'

'At least he had sense enough not to tell you! I always knew he'd crush that Vulture one day, just like he'd have crushed a wasp that stung him. You say Costantino is a good man? Well, my girl, you should have some idea what hatred is by now. Wouldn't you kill the men who've convicted Costantino? Yes or no? Yes, he killed the Vulture, and up to a point I sympathize with him, because I understand the workings of the human heart. But I don't forgive him, and I'll never forgive him his rashness. For the love of God, he has a wife and a son. If he had to do it, he should have gone about it more carefully. And now that's enough of that. You are still young, Giovanna. You must think of him as dead.'

'But he's not dead!'

'Very well, then,' said Bachisia, raising her voice. 'Go and hang yourself! You see that tree over there? Go and hang yourself from it, but don't torment me any more! You're the plague of my life, and you always have been. If you had married Brontu Dejas, you would have been all right. But no, you wanted that pauper. Well, just go and hang yourself!'

Giovanna did not reply. In her heart, she too believed Costantino was guilty, but she had long since forgiven him.

20

Her grief closed her mind to everything but Costantino's sentence. She could not comprehend how plain, simple men could thus dispose of the life of a fellow man.

On they rode. They had crossed the valley and were climbing the mountain on the other side. The sun sank, the horizon widened, the countryside lost its look of utter desolation. Long shadows stretched down from the mountain tops carpeting the low scrub, where a few dog-roses still bloomed. A slight breeze sprang up, filling the air with wild scents. Everyone's spirits lifted at the sudden shade and coolness. One of the company, joining the two women, began to tell a story about a strange adventure that had once befallen a friend of his in that very place. At one point the story became so racy that Giovanna even gave a faint smile.

The sun began to set, and from high up in the mountains the sea could be seen like a streak of bluish smoke on the clear horizon. Beyond the moorland vegetation that was so tough it withstood the ravaging winter winds and the scorching summer suns, high on the melancholy plain lost in a sea of light and solitude, stood Orlei, the tiny village where the Era family lived, a place full of rough, sturdy people, who made a living herding sheep and cultivating corn and honey.

Green pastures – dotted with rocks and in spring with clumps of asphodel, and fragrant with mint and thyme – and wheatfields met and hemmed in the little cluster of slate-stone cottages that gleamed like burnished silver. Here and there huge trees spread their shade over a quail's nest hidden in the corn. In the far distance lay green rows of tamarisk, thickets of thyme and arbutus, and the limitless stretches of the high plain itself, spread out under a sky of indescribable softness and sadness. On the right, against that same sky, blue in the morning, mauve in the afternoon, and violet or bronze in the evening, the mountains rose like huge sphinxes, their sides covered by forests, alive with eagles and vultures.

The Era women and their companions reached the village towards evening, when Monte Bellu, huge and mysterious like a sphinx colossus, was growing violet against an ash-grey sky. The village was already silent and deserted. On the rough paving of the streets the horses' hooves resounded like a shower of stones.

The company dispersed, and the two women went on alone to their own cottage, which stood in an open space above the level of the street. Another house, wearing a coat of whitewash, overlooked it. A large almond tree, growing beside the dry stone wall of the Era courtyard, hung over the street below, where the open fields began. Here and there on the bare patch under the almond tree, in front of the Eras' dark cottage and the Dejas' white one, large stones had been placed to serve as seats. This bare space became a kind of common courtyard shared between all the neighbouring houses.

As soon as she arrived, Giovanna dropped down from the horse, and with lagging step and hanging head approached a woman, a relative whom they had left in charge of the house, who came forward with a baby in her arms. Giovanna took the child from her, hugged him to her breast, and began to weep, burying her face on the innocent little shoulder. She wept quietly, deep in despair. It seemed to her that her former grief was nothing to that which she now felt. The baby, who was scarcely five months old, with unformed features and large glowing violet eyes, wore a red bonnet, whose fringes hid his forehead. He had recognized his mother, and was pulling very hard on the edge of her kerchief, kicking his two little feet and crying.

'My Malthinu, my little Malthinu, my only joy in the world, your papa's dead,' sobbed Giovanna.

The woman, understanding that Costantino had been found guilty, began to weep with her. Bachisia descended on the two of them, pushed Giovanna into the cottage, and asked the woman to help her unload the horse. Then she said in a low voice:

'Must you two carry on that way right here in sight of the white house? I can see Malthina's face, the nosey old hag. She's probably delighted to hear of our bad luck.'

'Oh no,' said the woman. 'She's been here several times to inquire about Costantino, and she seemed very sorry. She told me she'd dreamed they'd given him hard labour.'

'She's as sorry for us as a dog with rabies. I know her, she's a venomous snake, and she'll never forgive us because Giovanna turned Brontu down.' She added, moving to the door, the saddlebag over her shoulder, 'However, she's right, we'll never forgive ourselves either.'

Martina Dejas was the owner of the white house and the mother of Brontu Dejas, who had asked for Giovanna's hand and been refused. Martina was quite comfortably off, but a miser, and Bachisia was quite wrong in thinking that the woman hated her. Old Signora Dejas had not cared one jot about the refusal.

'Do me one more favour, Maria Chicca,' Bachisia said when the horse had been unloaded. 'Take the horse back and tell Martina that Costantino has been sent to prison for twenty-seven years, then watch the expression on her face.'

The woman took hold of the bridle – the horse had been hired out from the Dejas – and led it to the white house. This house, which had formerly belonged to a merchant who had gone bankrupt, had been bought at public auction a few years before. It was big and comfortable, with a portico that would not have disgraced a gentleman's house. In this portico, Martina let piglets and chickens wander about. The house did not suit rough shepherds like the Dejas, and the crude furniture, the hard, high wooden beds, roughly carved wooden coffers, benches, and heavy chairs, bore evidence of this.

Martina sat in the portico still spinning (she could even spin in the dark) when Maria Chicca brought back the horse. The house was empty, since Brontu and the farmhands were off at the sheepfolds, and Martina had no house servants. She had other sons and married daughters with whom, thanks to her miserliness, she lived in a state of constant dissension. When there was a lot of work to do in the house she summoned neighbours, often Giovanna and her mother, and paid them meanly with stale or damaged farm produce. These people were so poor that they were happy to get anything.

'Well, how did it go?' Martina asked, putting down the spindle and the little distaff on the portico bench. She had a thin, nasal voice, round, black close-set eyes, a thin hooked nose, and a mouth that was still pink and fresh. 'Have you been crying, Maria Chicca? I saw those two poor women arrive, but I didn't dare go to them, because last night I dreamed that they had sentenced Costantino to hard labour.'

'You've already told me that, Malthina. He got twenty-seven years.'

Martina seemed disappointed, not because she hated Costantino but because she thought her dreams infallible. Taking the horse's bridle, she said, 'If I can I'll go and see them this evening, but I don't know if I can because I'm waiting for a man who was one of Basilio Ledda's labourers. He's going to come and work for me. He was a witness at the trial, but I think he should be back from Nuoro by now.'

'I think he is,' said the other woman, going off. As soon as she got back to the cottage she told Bachisia and Giovanna that Martina felt very sorry for them, that the old woman had dreamed Costantino had been sentenced to hard labour, and that she had also said that Giacobbe Dejas, a distant and poor relation, was coming to work for the Dejas.

Giovanna was nursing the baby, her sorrowful eyes fixed on him, and she did not even raise her head. Bachisia, however, wanted to know all sorts of things: if the old Signora Dejas was alone; if she was spinning; if she was spinning in the dark.

'She might come by this evening,' she said to Giovanna.

Giovanna neither replied nor looked up.

'Didn't you hear me, my girl?' cried the mother angrily. 'She's going to come by here this evening.'

'Who?' asked Giovanna, as if waking from a dream.

'Malthina Dejas.'

'Her? To hell with her.'

'To hell with who?' asked a deep voice from the doorway. It was Isidoro Pane, an old leech-fisher, a relative of the Era family, who was coming to give them his condolences. Tall, with blue eyes and a long yellowing beard, he wore a carved bone rosary at his belt, and carried a long stick with a bundle fastened on the end. He looked like a pilgrim. He was the poorest, wisest and most serene of all the inhabitants of Orlei. If he ever wanted to swear at someone he would simply say,

'May you become a leech-fisher!'

He was a great friend of Costantino, with whom he had often sung the psalms of praise in church, and so the Eras had asked him to be a witness for the defence, since none better than he could attest to the good character of the accused. But his name had been rejected. What would the word of a poor leech-fisher amount to against the majesty of the law?

As soon as she saw him, Giovanna was so moved she began to sob again.

'God's will be done,' said Isidoro, leaning his stick against the wall. 'Have patience, Giovanna Era, do not lose faith in God.'

'Do you know what's happened?' asked Giovanna.

'I know, I know. But he's innocent, and I tell you that even though they have condemned him today, tomorrow he will prove his innocence.'

'Ah, Isidoro,' said Giovanna, shaking her head. 'I don't have your faith any more. I had faith up until yesterday, but now it's gone.'

'You're not a good Christian. These are the teachings of Bachisia Era.'

Bachisia, who viewed the fisherman with some distaste and was always afraid of his leaving some horrible vermin in the house, turned and was about to hurl abuse at him when another visitor arrived, followed by a woman and then a crowd of people. Soon the cottage was full, and even though she was by now tired out with crying, Giovanna felt obliged to start sobbing and shrieking again.

All the while, Bachisia was waiting for Martina Dejas, but the rich neighbour did not come. Instead, Giacobbe Dejas, who had just contracted to work for Martina, appeared alone. He was a cheerful man of about fifty, small and lean, clean-shaven, with neither eyebrows nor hair but with small, shrewd slanted eyes of a nondescript colour between green and yellow. He had worked for Basilio Ledda for twenty years; he had been called as a witness for the defence, recounting Basilio's ill-treatment of his nephew, and telling how on the day before he died, the old miser, who ill-treated servants and women as well, had beaten and kicked him – Giacobbe Dejas.

'Malthina is expecting you,' said Bachisia. 'You'd better . . .'

'The devil cut off her nose,' replied Giacobbe. 'I'm afraid I'm falling out of the frying-pan into the fire. She's a worse miser than *he* was.'

'If she pays you, you shouldn't criticize her,' said a deep voice.

'Oh, so you're here, Isidoro,' said Giacobbe, scornfully. 'How are things with you? How are your legs these days?'

Isidoro looked at his legs, which were wrapped in rags. To catch leeches he had to stand in stagnant water until the leeches fastened on to him, puncturing his skin.

'Never mind about them,' he said. 'You have no business to curse the woman whose bread you eat.'

'I eat my own bread, not hers. But that's enough about us. Well, Giovanna, bear up. Remember the story I told you on the way back from Nuoro? Be sensible, keep going for the sake of this brat. Costantino won't die in prison, I tell you. Give me the baby.' He leaned down, but seeing the baby was asleep, he straightened up and put a finger to his lips. 'Bachisia, please send your daughter to bed. She's exhausted. Friends,' he said to the others who were standing around, 'let's all do something to help. Let's be off now.'

One by one they all went. Then Bachisia picked up the stool on which Isidoro had sat, carried it outside and wiped it. When she came in she found that she had to shake Giovanna, who had dozed off, and make her go to bed. The girl opened her reddened, tear-filled eyes and got up, the baby in her arms.

'Go to bed,' ordered her mother.

The girl looked at the door, murmuring, 'He won't come back. He'll never come back. For a moment I felt I was waiting for him to come home.'

'Go to bed, go to bed!' said her mother in a harsh voice. She gave Giovanna a push, took down the old brass lamp, and opened the door. The cottage consisted of a kitchen with the usual stone hearth in the middle and an oven in one corner and two poorly furnished rooms. Giovanna's bed was a wooden board, high and hard, with a pink cotton bedspread. Bachisia took little Martino, who whimpered in his sleep, and put him down on the bed, cradling him in her hands while Giovanna got ready. When Giovanna lay in bed, bare-headed, her lovely hair flowing loose, her mother covered her carefully and went out.

As soon as Bachisia left the room, the girl pushed back the covers and began to cry. She was exhausted with grief and fatigue, her eyes were heavy with sleep, but she could not rest. Confused images passed through her mind, and as if her anguish were not enough, sharp stabs of acute pain shot through her teeth and temples. At times it seemed as if boiling water were being poured over her, and she felt an inexplicable terror.

The door was ajar, and from the next room Bachisia heard Giovanna sobbing and muttering, now addressing passionate words to Costantino and then threatening death to the jurors who had condemned him. Bachisia lay wide awake, her mind racing, going over all that had taken place and that would take place now. She resented Giovanna's grief but at last she too fell to weeping.

IV

The following day, towards evening, Brontu Dejas returned from the fields and no sooner had he dismounted than he began to grumble. He always grumbled at home, though with outsiders he was cheerful. He was a jovial handsome young fellow, very slim and dark, with a short, red, curly beard. He had fine teeth, and when he spoke to women he smiled continually to show them off.

Coming home now, he began to grumble because his mother had neither lit the lamp nor prepared the supper. He had reason to complain, for he was after all a labourer, and after a week of hard work, when Saturday came around, he returned to the village to find the house as dark and dirty as a beggar's hovel.

'Hey, this looks like Isidoro Pane's house,' he said, unloading the saddlebags. 'Light the lamps at least. You can't even see enough to swear. What's there to eat? Stones?'

'There are eggs and bacon, my son,' said Martina. 'Be patient. Did you know that Costantino Ledda has been sentenced to thirty years?'

'Twenty-seven. Well, what about those eggs? That bacon's rancid, Mother. Why don't you throw it to the chickens? The chickens, you hear,' he repeated, clenching his fine teeth in anger.

'They won't eat it,' Martina replied calmly. 'Yes, twenty-seven years. Twenty-seven years is a long time! I dreamed he had been condemned to hard labour.'

'Have you been round to see those two women yet? They must be pleased now with that fine marriage of theirs, those

28

filthy beggars,' he said. But as soon as his mother replied that yes, she had been there, that Giovanna was in despair, tearing her hair, and that Bachisia had given her to understand that she regretted not having strangled her daughter before allowing that marriage, Brontu flew into a rage.

'Why did you go over there? What business had you to go near that flea-bitten hole?'

'Ah, my son, you know nothing of Christian charity. The priest, Father Elias, was there this morning too. Yes, he went to comfort them. Giovanna wants to take the baby to Nuoro so that Costantino can see it before he's carried off. I told her it would be madness in this heat. But Father Elias told her to go, and he nearly cried.'

'What does he know about babies? He's sterile, like all of them,' said Brontu, who hated priests because one of his uncles, the parish priest of the town, had left his property to a hospital. Martina too still felt bitter about this, but the old vixen managed to conceal her resentment, and every time Brontu railed against priests she made the sign of the cross.

'What did you say, idiot? You don't even know where you're putting your feet. Father Elias is a saint. If he hears you speak like that – you'd better watch out. He has holy books, and he can put a curse on our fields and bring the locusts and make the bees die.'

'Fine saint!' remarked Brontu, then he insisted on hearing how Giovanna had cried out and what the old bitch Bachisia had said.

Indeed, Giovanna's weeping was enough to melt stones and Bachisia was in despair, because now, on top of everything else, the lawyer's fees and legal expenses had stripped them of everything they owned, even the cottage.

The young man listened intently, happy, showing his fine boyish teeth. He was fierce in his happiness.

'Giacobbe Dejas will be here in a short while,' said Martina. 'He wanted to start work tomorrow, but I told him to wait until Monday. It's a holiday tomorrow. Perhaps he can scrounge a meal somewhere.'

'San Costantino himself, you're a mean one, Mother.'

'You're just a child still! What's the point of wasting things? Life is long and it costs a lot of money.'

'And how are those two women going to live?' asked Brontu, after a moment of silence, sitting down to the dish of bread and eggs Martina placed before him.

'They'll have to catch snails!' said Martina ironically. She picked up her spindle again and set to work beside the open door. 'You're showing a lot of interest in those women, Brontu Dejas!'

Silence. The distaff and Brontu's strong teeth chewing the hard bread were the only sounds in the room. Outside, beyond the portico, the crickets chirped and from farther away in the solitude of the scrub, in the hot darkness of the evening, came the melancholy cry of an owl.

Brontu took a glass and filled it with wine. He opened his mouth, but not to drink. He wanted to say something to his mother, but the words would not come. He drank. With the back of his hand he wiped the drops that clung to his red beard, then lowered his eyes and opened his mouth again to speak. Still he could not.

A sound of footsteps was heard crossing the open space before the house. Martina got up, still spinning, and told her son that Giacobbe Dejas was coming. She picked up the food and the wine and put them away in the cupboard.

As he entered the room Giacobbe noticed what the old woman was doing and realized she was hiding the wine so as not to have to offer him a glass. But he was too much a man of the world (so he said) to be offended, and he came forward smiling and cheerful.

'I bet you're talking about me.'

'No. We were talking about poor Costantino Ledda.'

'Oh, yes, the poor fellow!' said Giacobbe, becoming serious. 'To think that he's innocent. Innocent as the sun. No one knows it better than me.'

Brontu leaned back at his ease, legs crossed, and showed his teeth as he did when talking to a woman.

'Opinions differ,' he said in a nasal voice. 'My mother, for example, dreamed they had sentenced him to death.'

'You mean to hard labour!'

'Same thing. Let's talk about our own business.'

They talked and made arrangements for the contract. Then the two men left together, and Brontu led the new servant to the tavern. Brontu was not mean. When someone called to see him, Brontu would never offer a glass of wine, as that would have angered his mother. Instead he would take his guest to the tavern and there would treat him very generously. That evening he made Giacobbe drink a lot and Brontu drank so much himself that they both became drunk.

As they walked up the dark, quiet street to where it met the harsh scent of the fields, they began to talk about Costantino again. Brontu said cruelly that he was pleased about the sentence.

'Go to hell,' cried Giacobbe. 'You're heartless.'

'All right. I'm heartless.'

'Because Giovanna didn't want you, you're glad to hear of the death, or worse than death, of a man like yourself.'

'Costantino's not dead, and he's not like me. As for Giovanna Era, it was I who didn't want her. If I had wanted her she would have licked the soles of my shoes.'

'Hmm. Pride comes before a fall, my chicken. You lie like a serving-maid.'

'I? I'm no serving-maid,' cried Brontu, enunciating the words clearly. 'If you say that to me again, I'll bash your head in.'

'I'll say it again then. You'll come to grief, my chicken.'

Their voices rang out in the night. Then they grew quiet, and silence fell again. In the distance, in the light of the stars that crowned the black profile of the mountains like garlands of golden flowers, the donkey answered the owl's melancholy cry. All at once Brontu began to weep in a weird, drunken way with neither tears nor sobs.

'What's the matter with you?' said the other man in a low voice. 'Are you drunk?'

'Yes, I'm drunk. Drunk with poison. I hope you strangle yet, you gallows bird.'

The other man grew indignant, not only because he had never been to prison but because of the suggestion that he had committed any offence. However, his voice was anxious when he asked, 'Have you gone mad? What's the matter with you? Why are you talking like that? What have I done to you?'

Brontu began to groan, as if one of his limbs were hurting, and he said that he loved Giovanna madly and that he had prayed to the devil that Costantino would be found guilty.

'Let the devil take my soul, I don't give a damn. I don't believe in him,' he said, and he laughed a harsh laugh that was sadder than his previous maudlin outburst. 'I'm going to marry Giovanna.'

Giacobbe was astonished at this, but he pretended to be even more astonished than he was.

'I think I'm going to choke,' he said. 'What do you mean by that? How can you marry Giovanna?'

'She'll get a divorce, that's how. There's going to be a law saying any woman whose husband has been sentenced to a long prison term will be allowed to remarry.'

Giacobbe had already heard about this law and, so as not to look ignorant, he said, 'Oh yes, I know. But it's a mortal sin. Giovanna will never do it.'

'That's what worries me, Giacobbe Dejas. Will you talk to her about it? Tomorrow perhaps.'

'Oh yes, tomorrow! You're a fool, Brontu. You may be rich but you're as stupid as a lizard. In fact you're stupider. You could marry a rich young girl, someone as fresh as a wild rose, and you want to marry that woman. You make me laugh.'

'Well, you can laugh until you split in two. I'm going to marry her,' said Brontu, furious again. 'There's no woman like her. You'll see. I'll marry her.'

'Marry her then, my little spring chicken,' replied the other man, laughing. Brontu began to laugh as well, and they laughed together for a long time, until they saw a tall man with a long stick coming quietly towards them.

'Isidoro Pane, how's the fishing?' asked Giacobbe. 'Are your legs full of holes?'

'May you become a leech-fisher yourself,' said the old man. 'What a smell of grappa! Someone must have broken a cask around here.'

'Do you mean you think we're drunk?' demanded Brontu threateningly. 'It's only because you can't afford it that you don't get drunk yourself. Go away or I'll kill you. I'll squash you like a frog.'

The old man laughed softly and walked on.

'Fool,' said Giacobbe. 'He could be your go-between. He's a friend of hers.'

Brontu turned, and gesticulating with his arms, called out, 'Come back. Come here, I tell you.

If you don't come here, you silly old man

Dogs will bite you whenever they can.'

Brontu laughed but Isidoro Pane paid no attention. 'Do you hear me?' called the drunken man, beginning to stammer. 'I'm telling you to come here. So you don't want to come here, you toad. I'll give you – '

But Isidoro only walked on, his footsteps soundless.

'Don't talk like that. What sort of a way is that to carry on?' muttered Giacobbe.

'Come here, little flower,' said Brontu, changing tactics. 'Come here, I want to tell you something. Tell that woman, your friend – you know, Giovanna – tell her she should divorce that husband of hers.'

At that the old man stopped, turned round, and called out in a clear voice, 'Giacobbe Dejas!'

'What do you want, my sweet?' said the shepherd sarcastically.

'Make him keep quiet,' replied Isidoro, meaning to be obeyed.

For a reason he could not explain to himself at the tone of that voice, Giacobbe took his master by the arm and drew him away, murmuring, 'What a fool you are. What sort of tactics are those? You're behaving like an idiot, my chicken.'

'Me? You're talking rubbish. I'm not a fool.'

They staggered on, arm in arm. In the Dejas' portico they found Martina still spinning in the dark. She saw at once that her son was drunk, but she said nothing because she knew that when he was in that condition the least thing could send him into a rage. When Brontu asked for wine, however, she said there was none.

'So there's no wine in the Dejas house, the richest house around? How mean you are, Mamma!' Then he began to bluster, 'I won't cause a scandal, no, but I am going to marry Giovanna.'

'Yes, yes, you're going to marry her,' said Martina, to soothe him. 'Now go to bed and keep your voice down, because if she hears you she won't have you.'

He quietened down, but he made Giacobbe spread two rush mats out on the floor. Then he lay down on one and made the shepherd lie down beside him. Rather than have any trouble Martina left them alone, and so it was that Giacobbe began his service on the Saturday night instead of the Monday.

V

One Sunday morning a fortnight later the whole village was assembled at a mass celebrated by the parish priest.

Giovanna alone was not there, and this was for two reasons. First, her plight placed her in a kind of mourning, which prevented her from showing herself outside the house except when her work made it necessary. But the main reason was because she had fallen into a sort of apathy that prevented her from moving, from going out, from working or praying. She had never been a devout Christian, but before the trial she had made a vow to walk barefoot and bareheaded to a certain church in the mountains, and, if Costantino were acquitted, to drag herself on her knees from the point where the church first came into view from the pathway, a distance of about two kilometres.

Now she neither prayed, nor spoke, nor ate. She also seemed to have lost all interest in her baby, and Bachisia had to feed him with bread mashed up in milk to keep him alive. Some said that Giovanna was going mad, and, indeed, when she came out of her apathy, crouched in a corner hour after hour with her glazed eyes fixed on the void, it was only to fly into a rage, tearing her hair and screaming out unintelligible words. After her last meeting with Costantino, when she had taken the baby with her, she could think of nothing else, and went on talking about the prison in the wild tones of a person obsessed.

'He was laughing. He was pale, and he laughed. Behind the bars. Malthineddu clung to the bars, and Costantino clutched the baby's hands. He laughed. Oh God! Oh God! Don't laugh like that! It hurts me, for I know that your laugh is the laugh of

35

the dead. And the warders stood there like vultures. At first they were kind, those warders of human flesh, but later, after Costantino had been convicted, they were cruel. Cruel as dogs. Malthinu was afraid, and he cried when he saw them. And his father laughed, do you understand? The baby, the innocent creature, cried. He understood that his father had been convicted, and he cried. Oh my God! Oh my God!'

'Dear love, Giovanna! You're behaving like a two-year-old child,' Bachisia fumed, having had enough of it. 'Your son has more sense than you, you fool.' She even made as if to hit the girl. But nothing – prayers, sympathy, threats – nothing had any effect.

Meanwhile, word came from Nuoro that while awaiting the appeal, Costantino had been transferred to a gaol in Cagliari. Then came a short, sad letter from him. He said the journey had gone well but Cagliari was suffocatingly hot, and certain red insects, and others of various colours, tormented him night and day. He sent a kiss to the child, begged Giovanna to bring Martineddu up in the fear of the Lord. He also sent greetings to his friend Isidoro.

On this Sunday, then, after the mass, Bachisia waited for the poor fisherman to finish singing the sacred psalms in his deep voice, so as to give him Costantino's message.

Father Elias remained on his knees on the altar steps, his face pale and ecstatic, praying. Isidoro went on singing, but the congregation began to file out.

Martina passed Bachisia walking haughtily like an old but still unbroken mare. Next came Brontu in his new suit, his hair slicked down with oil; then came Giacobbe, wearing a pair of rough new linen trousers that still smelled of the shop. Isidoro sang on.

The mass ended; the church was empty but still he sang. His deep voice resounded from the dusty white walls, from beneath the roof beams and reed ceiling, and among the lowly altars, covered with coarse cloth and decorated with paper flowers, watched over by melancholy saints of painted wood.

When he finished singing, there was no one left except the priest, a boy who was extinguishing the candles, Bachisia, and an old blind man. Once more Isidoro repeated the final response of the psalm and then he got up and put away the bell that was used to signal the reciting of the rosary. Bachisia stood waiting for him at the door. They went out together, and she gave him Costantino's message, then she asked him a favour. It was to ask the priest if he would consent to see Giovanna and reason with her about the state she had fallen into. He promised to do so, and in the street Bachisia was joined by Giacobbe Dejas.

'How are you?' asked the shepherd.

'Oh God, we are ill yet not ill! And you, how do you find your new masters?'

'I've already told you! I've jumped out of the frying-pan into the fire. The old woman's as mean as the devil. She expects me to work until I drop, and she scarcely allows me to come into town once a fortnight to hear mass.'

'And your master?'

'Oh, the little master? He's an animal, what else can I say?'

'What do you mean by that, Giacobbe?'

'Well, it's the truth, my chicken. He flares up like a mad dog at the slightest thing, gets drunk, and is as unpredictable as the weather. I suppose Isidoro Pane told you – ' He stopped uncertainly, and Bachisia, fixing her little green eyes on him, thought that if he spoke ill of his master he must have some reason.

'Look,' he went on, 'Isidoro Pane must have told you – of course he did – about Brontu being drunk that night. It was right here, on this spot, that he began to shout, "Tell Giovanna Era that if she gets a divorce I'll marry her!" He's an animal! A real animal! He drinks grappa by the barrel.'

From all this, Bachisia managed to grasp one thing, the fact that Brontu had said he would marry Giovanna if she got a divorce. Her green eyes sparkled, and she said haughtily, 'And you, Giacobbe – wouldn't you want that?'

'I? What do I matter, my chicken? But you should be ashamed of yourself to speak of such things, you old kite, barely two weeks after – '

'I'm no kite,' shrieked the old woman. Giacobbe laughed, but angrily.

37

'At least wait until after the appeal, then you can devour Costantino as you devour a harmless lamb. Devour him then, but Giovanna will marry a bottle of grappa and you, as long as Martina Dejas lives, you'll starve worse than ever.'

'Oh, you bald head,' Bachisia began, but Giacobbe walked quickly away, and she had to content herself with hurling a stream of abuse after him.

Not that she had any thought of getting her daughter to apply for a divorce – Heaven forbid! – with poor Costantino still under appeal, shut up in a burning furnace, eaten alive by filthy insects! No, but why did this horrible man say these things about his master? Why did he meddle in his master's affairs? Perhaps the bald old crow himself fancied Giovanna. Filled with these spiteful thoughts, she went back into the cottage.

She wanted to tell Giovanna everything, but finding her for the first time in two weeks bathed and combing her long dishevelled hair that tumbled about her, Bachisia dared not say a word.

VI

Time passed, autumn came and then winter. Costantino's appeal, as appeals always are, was rejected. One night he was bound by a length of chain to another convict, whom he had never seen before, and put in line with other men, two by two, all dressed in coarse clothes, all like beasts tamed by an unseen power. They marched, but where they did not know. They were silent, but why they did not know. They were driven down to the water's edge, put on board a long, black steamer and there they were shut into a cage.

Costantino was resigned. He was going towards a cruel and unknown fate, but he never despaired, for at the bottom of his heart he was convinced he would soon be freed. The bustle of passengers and crew, the clank of the chains, the steamship's first motion as it got under way aroused a childlike curiosity in him. He had never been on board a ship before. Sometimes, as a boy, he had scanned the horizon gazing at the ash-grey strip of the Mediterranean, dotted here and there by the wing of a sail. He had dreamed of crossing those faraway seas to unknown lands, to the golden cities of the mainland. He could read and write, and from the prints in a schoolbook he knew of St Peter's in Rome and of the ancient city of Jerusalem. Whenever from among the thickets of Monte Bellu he had gazed out at the grey line of the Mediterranean, it was to Jerusalem that he thought to go. Now, here he was crossing the sea, but how different from his dreams it was! Yet so splendid was Jerusalem to him that if it had been there he were going, even as a chained and convicted prisoner sentenced to expiate a crime, he would have been happy.

The steamer rolled and pitched as it ploughed on through the ceaseless crashing of the waves. The prisoners whispered among themselves, some joking and laughing. Costantino drowsed and dreamed, as he always did, that he was at home again. He had just been freed and he was returning home without letting his wife know, so as to give her the joy of surprise. Giovanna kept saying, 'But this is a dream, this is a dream!' The expenses of the trial had stripped the house bare of everything, even the bed. But that did not matter. All the riches of the world were nothing in comparison with the joy of liberty, the happiness of living again with Giovanna and Malthineddu. But Costantino felt tired, so he curled up in the baby's cradle, and the cradle was rocking, all by itself, faster and faster. Giovanna laughed and said, 'Careful you don't fall out, Costantino, my darling.' And the cradle rocked more and more violently.

At first he too laughed. Then all at once he began to feel ill, his head was spinning, and he fell from the cradle to the ground. He awoke feeling seasick. The sea was rough. The steamer climbed and plunged down over mountains of water. Waves broke over the third-class passenger deck.

All the convicts were ill. Some tried to go on making jokes, others cursed. Costantino's companion, a man with a smooth yellow face, whimpered like a baby.

'Oh,' he groaned clutching his drooping head in his hands and gasping with terror. 'I dreamed I was at home, and now – and now – dear St Francis, have pity on me!'

In spite of his own misery, Costantino felt sorry for the man. 'It's all right, brother, I too dreamed about being at home.'

'I'm dying, I'm dying,' moaned another. 'This ship is being sailed by demons. It's dancing a Sardinian jig!' At this some of the others even mustered the strength to laugh.

The storm raged all night and Costantino thought he was going to die. He was afraid of death, and yet life seemed to him entirely made up of grief. His soul seemed awash with the same bitter fluid that his stomach was casting up. Not even at the moment sentence had been pronounced on him had he experienced anything like this present feeling of hopelessness.

He too began to groan and curse, clenching his fists and twisting his chilled toes.

'I hope you die like I am dying now, you murderous dogs who brought this on me,' he said while tears as bitter as the liquid that poisoned his mouth and soul welled up in his eyes.

Towards dawn the storm subsided but even when the sickness had passed Costantino found no relief. He felt as if he had been battered to the point of death, and he shivered with cold, exhaustion, and fear. The steamer sailed on. If only it would stop for just one moment! A single moment would have been enough to restore Costantino's strength, but this endless pitching and tossing, this endless crash of waves went through him in a convulsive shiver. On and on they went, and after long hours of agony, night fell. The companion with the smooth yellow face went on moaning, driving Costantino into a frenzy of irritation. At last he was able to doze off, and he began to dream the same dream as on the first night. This time, however, Giovanna was angry, and the rocking of the cradle was almost gentle. When he awoke, he became aware that the steamer had stopped, and in the vast silence that precedes the dawn he heard a voice say, 'That is Procida.'

Shuddering with cold, he wondered if they were landing there, because that, he had heard, was where the galleys were. His companion woke too, shivering and yawning widely.

'Are we there?' asked Costantino. 'How do you feel?'

'Not bad. Have we arrived?'

'I don't know. We're near Procida. Is this where the galleys are?'

'No, they're at Nisida. But we're not going to the galleys!' said the other proudly, yawning again.

The prisoners were landed at Naples and immediately shut into a sealed black and yellow wagon that looked like a moving tomb. Costantino only caught a brief glimpse of a wide expanse of smooth green water, darkened by the shadows of enormous steamships, and boats laden with sleazy men shouting incomprehensible words. All round the boats on the surface of the green water floated vegetables, orange peel, bits of paper, and filth. Huge buildings stood out against a deep blue sky.

At Naples the prisoners were divided up. Costantino was taken off to the prison at X, and he never saw his sad companion with the smooth yellow face.

On reaching his destination, Costantino was at once shut in a cell where he was to pass the first six months of his term in solitary confinement. The cell was barely two yards long by two feet wide. There was nothing in it but a strange folding bed which, during the day, had to be closed and fastened to the wall. Through a little window the sky could be seen.

This was the dreariest period of his imprisonment. He sat motionless, hour after hour, legs crossed, hands clasped round his knees, but oddly enough he never lost hope or rebelled against his fate. He was convinced he was expiating that mortal sin, as he regarded it, of having lived with a woman to whom he had not been married in church. He still felt at the bottom of his heart the certainty that one day or another, after he had atoned for his sin, his innocence would be established and he would be set free.

Meanwhile, though he did not despair, he suffered. He counted the days, the hours, the minutes in the endless exhausting wait for some change that never came. Home-sickness dulled his mind and broke his heart. Day by day, hour by hour, minute by minute he relived his past life in his thoughts, recalling exactly each tiny detail of his distant home. And as well as his own grief he suffered Giovanna's. Transports of tenderness and love shook him from his pensive stillness, and then he would get to his feet and pace about. Because he could not take more than two or three steps, he would stop all of a sudden, and press his head against the wall. These were his moments of utmost desperation.

Then he went back to hoping, to weaving in his mind fantastic dreams of immediate and romantic liberation. Every time the warder entered his cell, Costantino's heart beat hard in expectation of some happy news.

Sometimes he played *morra* against himself, taking turns at being winner or loser. Afterwards he laughed at himself, like a child. On other occasions, he studied the palm of his hand at great length, imagining he saw a wide plain split up into smallholdings, with walls, rivers, trees, flocks of sheep, and shepherds, all of which he endowed with a life of exciting adventures.

Sometimes he prayed, counting on his fingers and singing hymns, experimenting and improvising new verses. In this way he actually composed a hymn of four verses, dedicated to San Costantino, in which he commended to the saint all prisoners wrongly condemned. The refrain ran:

'San Costantino, we beg mercy
For your condemned innocents!'

The composition of this hymn kept him occupied for many days, and made him almost happy. When it was finished he felt a deep joy, and the need to tell someone about it – but whom? The warder, a bald, little Neapolitan, with a shiny snub nose like that of a skeleton, would not understand the hymn. During the exercise hour it was strictly forbidden for the prisoners in solitary confinement to speak to their companions. So Costantino asked to confess himself, so as to be able to recite the hymn to the chaplain. The chaplain, who was young and intelligent, listened patiently to Costantino, making him translate the hymn. He then inquired if in asking to confess for the purpose of reciting his verses Costantino had not been guilty of the sin of vanity.

Costantino reddened and replied that he had not. The confessor smiled kindly, comforted him, praised the verses, and sent him away with a blessing.

A few days later the prisoner asked to confess again. 'Well, have you composed another hymn?' joked the chaplain.

'No,' said the prisoner, lowering his eyes. 'But I've come to ask a favour.'

'What favour? Tell me.'

Costantino paused for a moment, holding his breath, fearful of how much he might risk in making his request. Then he said quickly, 'I want to send the hymn to my home.'

'Ah,' said the chaplain. 'I can't help you. Anyway, how could you write it?'

'I know how to write,' exclaimed the prisoner, raising his clear eyes.

'Yes, but that was not what I meant, my brother. You are not permitted to write.'

'Oh, I'll get round that somehow.'

'Good, good, but I can't do anything for you.'

Costantino's face grew desolate and he could barely keep back the tears. Then he made his confession, asking if it would not be better to dedicate his hymn to Saint Peter and Saint Paul, since they too had been in prison, and he asked the chaplain's forgiveness if he presumed too much in making such a request.

The young chaplain gave him absolution, and prayed at length and out loud. Then, putting a hand over his eyes, he said slowly and softly, 'Write down the hymn, if you can do it. And have courage.'

A shudder of joy went through the prisoner, and from that moment he could think of nothing else but how he might write down his verses.

'I have been a student,' he told the warder one day. 'But I can also make shoes. Would you like me to make you a pair? They'll fit you well.'

'You're after something,' replied the little man in his Neapolitan dialect. 'You can't make anything.'

'Be a good fellow, Uncle Serafino. Think of your immortal soul.'

'I'm thinking of my soul, and I've already told you I'm not your uncle. You killed your uncle.'

'Oh well, no offence meant. At home we call all important people uncle.'

'My name is Don Serafino.'

But Costantino could not bring himself to call him that, because in Sardinia only the nobility bear the designation 'Don', so that day they came to no agreement.

Next day the prisoner brought up the subject again, saying that he came from a noble family, had received an education, and that his uncle, of whose murder he was accused, after having squandered the prisoner's own legacy, had forced him to work, to make shoes, and shut him in a dark room, and once had flayed all the skin from one of his feet. He wanted to show the foot, but Don Serafino shook his head with horror and under his breath cursed the dead man's cruelty.

Thus Costantino managed to obtain a sheet of paper, and with his blood he wrote down his hymn for the protection of convicted prisoners.

Winter came and went, and one day in March a portly man called by Costantino's cell on an inspection tour. The man had round, staring milky-blue eyes and such a short chin that his blond moustache completely covered it.

'You there,' he cried to the prisoner. 'What trade can you do?'

Don Serafino's skeleton face appeared among the party too, and seeing him the prisoner remembered the wild stories he had invented, and said that he knew how to make shoes.

Before long the warder told Costantino that he would soon be moved from his cell, shortening his term of solitary confinement. Costantino thought he owed this favour to his own good conduct, but Serafino told him in confidence that he had interceded for the prisoner to powerful people, for he believed Costantino really came from a noble family.

A few days later Costantino was put into a dormitory, and along with a number of other convicts he began work as a cobbler. He was also allowed to send word to Giovanna. He could write a letter every three months. All this made him almost happy. Then came spring, and the spirits of the convicts, who had suffered intensely from the cold, were greatly improved. In the shop where Costantino worked they were always joking. There were, however, two brothers who, having begged to be allowed to work together, quarrelled incessantly over some business deal they were trying to settle for after their release in ten years' time. One day they laid into each other, and one was taken away. They had to do two weeks in solitary and as soon as they saw each other again during the exercise hour – the hour of freedom that the convicts spent in the courtyard – they started to scuffle once more.

It was during that exercise hour that Costantino had become friendly with a fellow countryman, a Sardinian known as the King of Spades, perhaps because he had a triangular face, a large body and spindly legs. He was stout and pale and had had his head shaved so that he looked bald.

He was an ex-police inspector, convicted for embezzlement. He claimed to be related to a cardinal who was, in his turn, a friend of the king and queen. Thus, day after day, he expected a pardon, not only for himself, but he also promised a pardon for any convict who gave him cigarettes, money, or other things. Employed in the clerk's office and thus able to communicate with the outside world, he promoted a secret correspondence between the convicts and their families, and he managed to smuggle in money, tobacco, stamps and alcohol, thereby profiting greatly. He at once offered Costantino every favour and asked him if he wanted to send any letters home.

'Yes,' said the young man, 'but I have nothing to give you. I'm poor.'

'Never mind, we're fellow countrymen,' said the other man generously. He thereupon told Costantino tales of his gallantry as a police inspector, of how he had killed more than ten bandits, and how he had ten medals and had once been to Rome, where the king invited him into his box at the theatre. He was a hero. But he never spoke of his crowning feat. He only said he was in prison because of the machinations of certain jealous enemies. At the start, Costantino believed him and gave him every sympathy despite his ungainly appearance. Then, day by day, as the inspector's stories changed and became ever more exaggerated, he too – like the other convicts who despised the King of Spades but played up to him for their own ends – became sceptical.

It was soon obvious that all the prison inhabitants, including the warders, were liars and felons. The convicts had to hide their real selves and to make up fantastic stories about the past and the future that would enhance them in the eyes of their companions. Costantino noted with surprise that the convicts with the longest sentences were the least wicked, though the vainest and the biggest liars. Some of the lesser convicts bore grudges among themselves. They were mean, and they spied on each other. The long-term convicts made use of these petty criminals, betraying them as soon as they had served their purpose, betraying their friends without hesitation.

The King of Spades said to Costantino, 'Corruption gnaws deep into almost all the convicts, many of whom are dyed-in-the-wool criminals familiar with every form of vice. The very air we breathe is contaminated. If a man is cut off from society, deprived of his freedom, instead of suffering punishment he becomes completely sodden, loses what remains of his moral sense, turns into a liar so violent and so corrupt that he is no longer even aware of his own depravity.

'In my opinion,' he went on, 'the only honest men here are us two, Gooseneck, and the Delegate. All the others are criminals. Watch out for them, Costantino, old fellow. This is a clutch of bandits worse than those I've sent to the gallows.'

Costantino was horrified, reflecting that if his honesty bore any resemblance to that of the King of Spades there was small reason to be happy. Gooseneck, however, was a Sicilian student, a consumptive with white hair, a long neck, and a boy's body. He was always reading, he looked browbeaten, and scarcely spoke, but he was sometimes overcome by violent rages, after which he had to submit to the embraces of Ermelinda, as the prisoners called the straitjacket. He had once killed a professor. The Delegate was also a southerner, convicted for blackmail. He seemed a gentlemanly fellow, with a broad, prominent chest, a noble head, a large Grecian nose, and a cleft lower lip that jutted out. Scorn animated his face. If questioned, he too had great and powerful protectors, but he was persecuted by high-ranking people and especially by a minister. He had read a number of scientific books lent him by the student and was now engaged in writing a great scientific work, for he was employed in the clerks' office and could work for himself on the side.

The King of Spades was a great admirer of his. 'That man is going to make all our fortunes,' he would say to Costantino. 'We work on the book every day and we have a set of phrases of our own, referring to it. But we have to be careful, or woe betide us, we'll wreck all his work, which is a real piece of scientific discovery. I can tell you the main chapters in it. "How the

Atmosphere was Formed " – that is, the air. "How the Ocean was Formed" – that is, all the seas. "The Origins of the Organic World." – A rational demonstration of the existence of a primordial continent in the central region of the Pacific Ocean – Human life on this continent originated in that tropical region – Immigration to Africa and Asia – Disappearance of this continent as a result of a great cataclysm – Identification of this cataclysm with the Flood in the Bible – Emergence of the other continents – Then: End of the atmosphere. End of the ocean. End of the moon. End of the earth.'

'And the end of imprisonment?' asked Costantino, who had not understood very much and supposed the King of Spades was spinning his usual tall tales. But the King of Spades wanted to be listened to, and he went on dramatically.

'The other chapters are: "Amplification of the Accepted Doctrine of Evolution", "Evolution of Our Species from Anthropomorphic Apes", "Causes of the Inclination of the Axis of the Planets, Sun-Spots, etc.".'

'Go to the devil,' thought Costantino, yawning. Looking round the yard, with its fountain playing, he said, 'What about the magpie?' He was talking about a tame magpie that lived in the compound. It was fat and somnolent. When hungry, it would call one of them as if by name in a strange nasal voice.

'He'll kick the bucket,' said the King of Spades. 'Why worry about a bird? You're like a child, Costantino. You have no idea of the importance of the Delegate's work. Indirectly, I played a major part in his discovery. It was I who put him in touch with Gooseneck. We have already managed to get out a synopsis of the work, and we have written to the king's prime minister. But, remember! Not a word of this to anyone. One eminent scientist, who has read the synopsis, said: "It is one of the loftiest examples yet of Italian genius!" Believe me, Costantino, my dear fellow, the Delegate has climbed to dizzy heights. He has powerful friends who are now in Rome, working to obtain a pardon for him, but he has powerful enemies as well. However, this work will win him freedom.'

Costantino found this talk tiresome, but he pretended to listen with interest so as to remain in the other's good graces, for he was waiting for a reply to a letter he had written to Giovanna.

The reply came in May, filling Costantino with joy. Giovanna wrote that the baby had been ill, perhaps because her anxieties had dried up her milk, but now he was well. Isidoro Pane had received the hymns to San Costantino written in blood, and had wept when he read them and was going to sing them in church, accompanied by the whole congregation. No one knew where the verses came from, but Isidoro said he had received them from an old man with a long white beard, dressed in white, who had appeared to him one day on the river bank. He believed it was San Costantino or even Jesus Christ himself. Giacobbe Dejas had hired himself out to his rich relatives, and the lawyer from Nuoro had taken possession of the title to their house, allowing the women to live in it for a low rent. The Dejas family often gave work to Bachisia and also to her, Giovanna, and thus they managed to get along. Pietro Pania had been ill with a carbuncle and died. Annicca, who was known as Silver Shoulders, had got married. An old shepherd had been arrested for stealing beehives.

Almost all Giovanna's letters were full of such small titbits, which filled Costantino with satisfaction, pleasure, and interest. He felt as if he were breathing the air of his native land, seeing again the stones, the wild scrub, the people, the things to which his heart was most deeply attached.

The only thing that disturbed him was that Giovanna sometimes worked for the Dejas. He knew of Brontu's passion for her, of the rejected suit, and he felt a vague sense of apprehension. Giovanna sent him three lire hidden among the sheets of writing paper, and thinking that the money probably came from the Dejas he hated to touch it. Two lire of it he offered to the King of Spades, expecting his fellow Sardinian to refuse them. The man took them, however, saying they would be useful for paying the person who looked after the clandestine correspondence.

In other circumstances, Costantino would have been furious, but just then he felt such a need to write to Giovanna, to keep in touch with his far-off little world, that he would

49

have given half his life to secure the good office of the King of Spades.

He read and reread his letter until he knew it by heart. During the day he kept it hidden in the sole of his shoe, ripping it open each night and then stitching it up again the following morning. As he worked in silence, he thought constantly of the life and the people in the faraway little village. He identified so much with his dreams that he forgot reality. He imagined the old shepherd creeping carefully up to the hives, his face and hands wrapped in rags. The place was sunny and deserted. The green fields, spangled with dog-roses, honey-suckle, and sweet peas, stretched as far as the eye could see. In the vast silence, surrounded by the intoxicating scent of wild pennyroyal and other aromatic plants, the bees buzzed.

Anxiously Costantino followed the movements of the old thief. He saw him pull the little cork hives from the flat stones on which they stood, tie them together with a piece of rope, put them in a sack, and carry them off. As he was daydreaming in this way, a nasal voice broke in, calling 'Costanti! Costanti!'

Arousing himself from his dream Costantino saw the magpie hopping slowly round the yard, fat and round, fluttering its blue-black wings.

At night, with the letter under his cheek, he again took up the thread of his dreams. He heard the deep voice of his fisherman friend singing the hymn, and sometimes he wondered if on the river bank, among the swaying oleanders, with their sweet heavy bunches of pink flowers, Isidoro had not really seen the face of an old man, dressed in white, with a long white beard like the fleece of a new-born lamb.

Ah, San Costantino his guardian angel (whom Costantino imagined old and white-haired like a patriarch, even if the statue of the saint in the village church showed him as a warrior with a dark face), it was he who now came to Isidoro to tell him that he had not forgotten the unjustly condemned. The aged saint would soon grant him freedom. Blessed San Costantino!

Then the picture changed. It was the portico of the Dejas' house, where the spun wool was divided into long skeins preparatory to being woven. Back and forth went Giovanna with the huge skein in her hands. And there was Brontu, seated outside the kitchen door, legs apart, and between them, standing unsteadily and laughing, was little Malthineddu. Oh, horrible thought. But then Costantino remembered that Brontu was never in the village on working days, and he awoke with a start, his heart burdened with a feeling of mingled sorrow and joy.

VII

Summer came again.

'How quickly the time flies,' Martina said as she sat spinning under the portico. 'It seems only yesterday, Giacobbe, that you came to work for us, and here you are already renewing your contract. How time flies by for us poor landowners! You've saved up thirty silver *scudi* and are building yourself a house. What have we got to show for it?'

'How well you put it, Martina, my little chicken. What about my sweat? Doesn't that count for anything?' replied the shepherd, who was greasing a leather thong with tallow.

'What about your keep? Doesn't that count?'

May the crows pick your bones, thought Giacobbe, not daring to say it aloud. He hated his masters, the old miser and her hotheaded son, who was always going on about how he meant to marry Giovanna if she got a divorce. But Giacobbe wanted to renew his contract, and so he held his tongue.

He greased the thong, rolled it up, and hung it in the kitchen, and asked the old woman if he could go and see to a small business matter of his own.

'Go on, then,' she said reluctantly.

On his way down to the Eras' cottage, the shepherd came upon little Malthineddu astride a hobby-horse made of a length of reed. He was tottering along in his dirty white smock, his bare legs and arms tanned golden by the sun. The shepherd crouched down, spread his arms, and blocked the child's path.

'Where are you going? Don't you see the sun? It's going to scorch you up and carry you off. Run home.'

'No, no!' shrieked the child, jumping up and down on his horse.

'All right then, my little chicken,' went on Giacobbe, lowering his voice and casting a sideways glance at the portico. 'There's old Aunty Malthina. She's so mean that to save bread she eats little boys. D'you see her?'

The boy seemed convinced, and let himself be led back home, but he insisted on riding his hobby-horse.

Giovanna sat sewing in the doorway. She was as plump, rosy and fresh as if nothing had ever happened to her. Glossy black hair fell across her forehead. She looked up, and seeing Giacobbe with the child she smiled.

'Here you are,' said the shepherd. 'I'm bringing him back. He was out in the heat of the sun, on his way to Martina, who eats little boys instead of bread.'

'Go on with you!' said Giovanna. 'Don't say things like that to a child.'

'I say them to grown-ups too, because Martina eats them too. Watch out she doesn't eat you, Giovanna Era. You look so like a ripe peach. No, a peach is yellow. Let's see. You look like a . . .'

'A prickly pear!' she laughed.

'And how's Bachisia? When did you last hear from Costantino?'

At this, Giovanna's face grew serious, and she said, with an air of mystery, that she had not had any news from the prisoner for a long time.

'Is Isidoro Pane around? I must talk to him.'

'He's around,' she said, going back to her sewing.

Giacobbe walked off thoughtfully down the street towards Isidoro Pane's house – if the place could be called a house.

Isidoro, who fished for trout and eels as well as for leeches, when the opportunity presented itself, was seated in the shade of his hovel, mending a net. This hut stood out towards the fields a little apart from the rest of the village, and was a prehistoric structure made of small pieces of slate and roofed with cane and tiles, on which grew a reddish lichen.

The afternoon had been burning hot and the sun was now sinking. Not a leaf stirred on the dusty trees, rigid in the hot, empty village. Streaked here and there by slanting shadows, the yellow plain gasped in the blood-red sunset, and the distant, almost peacock-blue mountains and the huge purple-veiled sphinxes surged up into a fiery sky. In the vast silence a blackbird sang far off. Wild fig trees with hard, blackish leaves and a hedge of wild locust, in which were entwined tall hairy nettles and pale-leaved henbane, surrounded the fisherman's hovel. From the door, where he sat, the distant horizon lay as empty and misty as the sea. A strong smell of stubble and dry asphodel filled the air. Tree stumps, brushwood, bits of straw and dry leaves covered the earth, so that Giacobbe was able to approach silently, without Isidoro raising his head from his work.

'What are you doing?' Giacobbe said.

The fisherman looked up at Giacobbe but did not reply. Giacobbe sat beside him on the ground, legs crossed, and looked at the net the fisherman was sewing with a large, rusty needle.

'It looks to me,' Giacobbe laughed, 'as if the fish will be able to go in and out of that as they please.'

'Let them go in and out as they please, my little chicken,' replied Isidoro, imitating Giacobbe's phrase. 'Why are you in the village? Have you left your job?'

'No such luck. I've just made a new contract with those vampires, my rich relatives. But I want to talk to you about something important, Sidore. First, tell me how your legs are? And how long is it since you last saw San Costantino on the river bank?'

The old man frowned, because he did not like to hear holy things spoken of irreverently, and he answered in a low voice, 'If that's all you came for, you may as well leave now.'

'Don't get upset. I'll tell you why I came. It's something important. Anyway, if I've become a heathen, it's because of the young master, who's always slandering the saints, until he thinks he's going to die – then he's terrified. The other night we saw a star fall through the sky, straight to the earth. Brontu threw himself down on the ground screaming, "If this is our last night on earth, have mercy on us, Lord!" He lay there flat on his face. I wanted to kick him.'

54

'Weren't you afraid?'

'Not me, my chicken! I've often seen stars vanish.'

'Tell the truth. When you saw it move weren't you afraid?'

'Oh to hell with you. Of course I was. Anyway, I came to talk to you about my master. If he isn't mad, then no one is. He wants you to go to Giovanna Era and suggest she separate from her husband and marry him – Brontu.'

Isidoro stopped sewing. A shadow passed over his tranquil eyes. He clasped his hands together, leaned his chin on them and shook his head.

'Are you crazy coming here to tell me that,' he said in a deep voice. 'I understand. You don't want to lose your job. You're vile.'

'Hey!' cried the other man, pretending to be offended. 'Do you think you're talking to your leeches?'

'Oh, so you're joking? That's enough of that. Tell your master that's enough. The whole town is whispering.'

'My dear fellow, we've only just begun to talk and you want to stop. I've had a bellyful of it. Night and day he talks about it to me, the grappa barrel! I promised him I'd come and see you, so I came. But not as a favour to him. Only one person can stop this gossip – Giovanna. Go and tell her to silence the filthy dog, I can do no more.'

Isidoro gazed at him, apparently not listening to what he said. Then he took up his work again, murmuring, 'Poor Costantino, poor lamb, what have they done to you?'

'Yes, he's innocent,' said Giacobbe, 'and he'll come back one day. We must put a stop to this obsession of Brontu's. It's all Bachisia. She's hovering like a vulture over its prey.'

'Poor Costantino, poor lamb, what have they done to you?' went on the other man, without listening to Giacobbe.

The shepherd became angry. His voice rang out harshly in the great red silence, in the protective solitude of the fig trees and the wild hedgerows.

'They've made a cuckold of him! Why won't you listen to me, you old piece of filth? We must do something at once. That young woman is merry and fresh, and at the first proposal she'll fall like a ripe apple. She's not bad at heart, and if you want to help her, make her think of her duty and perhaps this disaster will be avoided. Go on. Get moving. If it's true you're a saint, like the fools say, work a miracle.'

The old man got to his feet. His tall majestic figure, draped in rags, loomed up like a hermit of old, against the wild background and the empty horizon.

'I'll go, I'll go,' he sighed. Giacobbe felt a weight lift from his heart. But the struggle the two men had taken on was to be a bitter one, ranged as it was against Brontu's ugly passion, Bachisia's greed, and Giovanna's indifference. Martina too no longer looked askance upon what her son intended. Giovanna was poor, but she was healthy and frugal, and she worked like a beast of burden. A well-off woman would be offended by the disorder and dissipation in the house, and a wedding would bring enormous expense. Giovanna, however, could have a secret wedding and come to the house as an unpaid servant.

Autumn came bringing sultry days, when the sea smoked on the horizon and dark, swollen clouds, like huge spiders, passed across the milky sky. The days were clear and cold.

In the evenings out in the fields, when the sky reflected the purple clouds and the wind carried the scent of thyme burned by the peasants who were breaking up the heathland to sow wheat, Brontu drank long gulps of grappa to warm himself. He lay in the shepherds' hut dreaming, warm and happy as a cat. Outside, around the hut for immense distances, the Dejas' *tancas** undulated, empty in the dusk. In and out of the golden stubble the earth burst, swollen with autumn rains, and from the pale green grass and the purple autumn flowers arose the scent of mushrooms. Flocks of black crows rustled out of the tarragon bushes, which looked like heaps of cinders, and flew to the woodlands of rock-roses and the tangle of wild strawberry trees, with their shiny leaves and pale gold berries.

On one of the *tancas*, the Dejas' farm labourers were burning the scrub, clearing the ground to plant barley and wheat. The flames crackled, the smoke spread out heavy with odours like

---

Tanca: an area of mountainous pasture land containing a shepherd's sheepfolds and his *ovile*, a small stone hut to shelter in. [Tr.]

the fumes of incense. The thorny hedges were sketched like purple embroidery against the silvery air. The flocks of sheep had been herded in, and only a few horses, muzzles to the ground, still grazed. Behind the hut could be heard Giacobbe's voice, a tinkling of sheep bells, the distant bark of a dog, and the harsh cry of a crow.

Inside the hut, stretched on warm skins and fleeces, like an Arab sheikh, Brontu pursued his unbroken sleep. The fiery liquor flooded his heart with its deep sweetness. It was rash to disturb him then. The sweetness would change into a bile bitter as gall. As a dog thumps its tail when pestered in its sleep, so he would flare up into a blind rage. His father too had loved hard liquor, and once when drunk he had fallen into the fire and died of his burns. But Brontu was more careful and anyway he had his passion for Giovanna to keep him safe. Grappa and Giovanna! The most beautiful, fiery, and intoxicating things in the world! But Brontu was timid with Giovanna even when he was inflamed by grappa. He trembled at the thought of approaching her, of speaking to her. On the days when he knew she was working for Martina, he was racked by the desire to return to the village, to see her in his house, to watch her. Then he would not dare leave the *tanca*. But time went by, and he was consumed by waiting and anxiety. He feared that if he delayed Giovanna would refuse him once again. He wanted to show her his concern for her, to tell her that he'd wanted to marry her at once, to look after her, the moment Costantino was convicted. He was good at heart, like all drunkards, and he was by nature honest. Since boyhood, when his family had come to live in the new house, his one passion, besides the grappa, had been Giovanna. She was fifteen then, fresh and beautiful. Every time he saw her, Brontu blushed to the roots of his hair, and she, realizing, was not offended. But he never spoke, and when finally he decided to send his mother to Giovanna's mother, the place had been taken. In those days Giovanna, proud and wild as a filly, did not understand the value of money, and just as she would have married Brontu Dejas for his fine teeth alone, so she would not have been false to Costantino even for the viceroy – had there still been one in Sardinia.

The twilight deepened. The sky became still clearer, and the clouds took on a purple colour, and grew long and as scaly as fish. Sounds and animal noises became more intense in the silence of the hour, and one evening Brontu dreamed that he heard Bachisia talking.

'St John the Baptist!' said a harsh, mournful voice. 'If I'm not mistaken, you're Giacobbe Dejas.'

'At your service,' came the somewhat surprised voice of the shepherd. 'What bad weather have you brought here, my little chicken?'

'At last. Where is Brontu Dejas?'

Brontu stumbled out of the shed. His legs were shaking and his head was spinning. As if through a mist he saw Bachisia's dark face. She carried her shoes in her hand and a bundle on her head.

'Bachisia,' he muttered. 'Here I am. Come in. Good evening.'

She all but hurled herself at him.

'Oh Brontu, dear son-in-law, if tonight isn't the death of me nothing will be. I've been walking for three hours. I lost my way. I must speak to you. Please listen to me.'

He did more than listen. He was moved almost to tears. He took her hand and led her into the hut. Giacobbe, who had followed behind, realized he was not wanted, and he retreated behind the hut, straining his ears and pacing up and down like a caged beast.

He could hear nothing. It was a short conversation and Bachisia would not even sit down. She said she had got lost near Brontu's sheepfold and that Giovanna, whom she had told to go and pick greens, must be waiting for her anxiously. They were forced to live on weeds, as they were so poor. Bachisia came to beg Brontu for money. If they could not pay it back to him, she and Giovanna would work for nothing for the Dejas until the debt was made good. They hadn't paid the rent for their house for many months, and the lawyer was threatening to evict them.

'Where can we go then, Brontu?' said Bachisia, wringing her yellow clawlike hands. 'Where can we go to, dear Brontu?'

Brontu's heart leapt in his chest. He would have liked to have thrown his arms round the old woman and cried, 'My house is yours,' but he dared not.

He had no money with him, so he decided to return to the village at once. He went out and called to Giacobbe to saddle the horse.

'What's happened?' asked the shepherd. 'Has your mother died, glory be to God?'

'No,' replied Brontu, without anger, 'nothing has happened that concerns you.'

Giacobbe saddled the horse, dying to know why Bachisia had come and why Brontu was returning to the village. Did she want money? He had none there. Was he going to get her some? 'Listen, Brontu!' he called. When the young man came up, he muttered, 'If that woman wants money and you haven't any, I'll give her some.'

'Yes, she wants money – urgently,' replied Brontu in a low, happy voice. 'I'm going back. Even if I had some here I'd go anyway, because this evening I can see Giovanna, I can go into her house. I'm going to speak at last. I'm going to do for myself what you, you fool, couldn't do.'

'You've gone mad, man!' exclaimed Giacobbe.

'All right, I've gone mad. Here, tighten these girths. You're pushing out your stomach, little horse,' he said to the animal. 'Don't you want an evening walk? What'll you do when the old woman's sitting on your crupper?'

'She too?' cried Giacobbe.

'She too, yes, so what? Isn't she my mother-in-law?'

'You're going too fast. Watch out you don't break your neck, my chicken. You're really serious, aren't you?' he gabbled. 'You want to marry that beggar, that married woman? You who could marry a flower of a young girl. Costantino Ledda is innocent. He'll come back, I tell you, he'll come back.'

'Leave me alone, Giacobbe. Mind your own business. Put a saddlebag on the crupper. Bachisia?'

Giacobbe ran into the hut and called to the woman to come out. 'Shame on you,' he said trembling with anger. 'You're worse than a beggar! I'll tell Giovanna, I'll tell her.'

'You're mad,' replied Bachisia, and cursed him in a low voice.

Shortly after, she and Brontu left. Giacobbe watched them recede into the distance over the lonely fields, away along the winding path beyond the scrub, beyond the smoke of the burning heath. In a spasm of helpless fury, he snatched his cap from his head and hurled it away, then he picked it up and belaboured the dog, who began to howl, filling the quiet evening with anguish. The lament came echoing back like the despairing plaint of a phantom.

Giacobbe went to lie down on the pallet Brontu had just left. He could smell the grappa. He found the master's bottle and drank. Then he went to sleep, and he too felt a smouldering in his breast, flooding his heart, bubbling up into his head, burning his eyelids. His anger fell away and sadness settled over him. From the door of the hut he could see the blood-red light of the burning heath slowly conquering the last, blue glimmer of dusk. Mingled together, the two took on a purple tinge of indescribable sadness. From time to time the dog whimpered. Why had he beaten the poor dog? He felt the drunkard's vague, tender remorse. At the same time the moaning irritated him, and he felt an urge to take it out on the poor animal again.

All at once he thought of Brontu and Bachisia, and he shivered. What would happen that night? Would Giovanna consent? Why did that dog keep whimpering? It sounded like the voice of the dead. The voice of Basile Ledda, that old murdered vulture. But the dead are silent. It's only the howling of a dog.

He began to laugh and to drowse. His eyelids closed. He no longer saw the misty, purple darkness that pressed against the entrance of the hut. He felt as if a sack of a soft, heavy material were falling over him. He could not move, but there was something sweet and pleasant about the stillness. Then he began to dream confused dreams. He dreamed he had died of a viper's bite and his soul had entered into the body of a dog, and this small, lean, yellow dog was sniffing round Bachisia's kitchen, looking for a bone. Costantino was sitting by the fireside. He was dressed in red with a huge chain round his

60

ankle. When he saw the dog he threw the chain at it. The animal's head was gripped in an iron ring and full of terror, Giacobbe forced himself to speak so he would be recognized. He awoke sweating, crying, 'Little chicken!'

It was midnight. Beneath a clear sky, full of huge golden stars, the deserted *tanca* glowed red with the burning scrub.

Unable to sleep, Giacobbe lay a long time tossing this way and that. The drunken euphoria had passed, leaving his mouth dry and bitter. He rose and drank. Then he remembered that the evening before he had eaten nothing, and he lay for a long while in the doorway of the hut, thinking, his face illumined by the firelight.

'Ought I to eat something?' he wondered without realizing what he was saying. He looked up at the stars. It was close to midnight. What had that little animal, the master, got up to? Giacobbe felt a new spark of anger, chiefly against Bachisia, who had boldly come with her crazy idea to beg from the young man. He knew it was just the old hag's ruse to catch Brontu, to make up his mind for him. She was a filthy old woman. She had no conscience. Didn't she believe in God? At that, Giacobbe Dejas became thoughtful. Then he lay down again, wondering if he was hungry and if he should eat.

No, he was not hungry or thirsty or sleepy. He could find no peace either lying down or sitting or standing. To distract himself a little he began to yawn widely and to babble aloud senselessly. He could not take his mind off *that thing*. It was horrible, horrible! Would it be possible to find a priest with so little conscience as to marry a woman already married? Anything could be done if you had money. What if Costantino came back? Even if the prisoner did not return, there was still his son. What would happen when the boy reached the age of reason? He would know his mother had two husbands. The newspapers were now reporting the imminent arrival of the new law on divorce. But what did the newspapers and the law count before God and a person's conscience?

Giacobbe rose, picking up the bottle of grappa. 'If Brontu asks who's been drinking his grappa, too bad. I'll tell him the moles drank it.' He laughed, drank, and lay down again. He went back to sleep and dreamed that one of his sisters had arrived, and he told her his dream about the dog, Costantino, and the chains.

When he awoke the sun had already risen over the edge of the high plain behind a line of bluish mist. The morning was a little cold and hazy. The heath, the scrub, the stubble, the moist green grass glinted with dew in the slanting rays of the sun. The birds rustled and sang so loudly in the bushes, that it sounded like a shower of crystal rain. The cawing of a crow rasped out against the background of that shimmering chorus. Then all sound died away into the intense silence of the plain.

Giacobbe went out, stretching and yawning. He yawned so widely that his jaws creaked. His face crinkled up around his open mouth, and his slanted eyes, yellow in the sun, watered like a dog's.

He pressed his hands to his stomach. 'I've got a pain here,' he said. 'What was I doing last night?'

He went over to the sheepfold and opened it up. The rams, with their twisted horns, came out sniffing the ground and a group of dirty sheep followed, butting each other. More came out. The sheepfold emptied, but Giacobbe remained beside the hedge, still and thoughtful.

'I didn't have anything to eat last night. I drank the master's grappa and I had a dream. Costantino and the dog, my sister Anna-Rosa. To hell with the little toad. Why hasn't he come back?' he thought, shaking his head. 'I got as drunk as a newt. A drunken man,' he said, going back to the hut, 'is like a beast. He no longer knows what he is doing. He shouts out whatever's in his mind at the top of his voice. It's bad for you, Giacobbe Dejas, you bald head, get that into your nut. If I ever drink any more, may God punish me.'

A short while after, Brontu returned. Giacobbe shot him a hard look and grinned. 'You look like a beaten man. What's happened, my chicken?'

'Nothing. Shove off.'

But the shepherd had no intention of going away. He circled round and round Brontu, nuzzling him like a dog, pestering, insisting on being told. Brontu told him everything – more than he needed to. Giovanna had shooed him away, just as if he'd been a tiresome beggar. She had asked him if he didn't realize she had a son who might one day spit in her face and ask why she had two husbands.

'Oh God, I knew it!' cried Giacobbe, jumping for joy.

'What did you know?'

'That Giovanna has a son.'

'I knew that too. Look, she threw me out. That's all there was to it. I could hear the mother and daughter arguing from out in the street.'

Then Brontu looked for his bottle of grappa. Giacobbe felt happy; he wanted to laugh. 'By the way,' he said, 'last night the mice drank your grappa. Ha, ha, ha! But there must be more. Look, here's some more.'

Brontu drank eagerly, without replying. Then he threw the bottle angrily at the shepherd, who caught it in mid-air. As Brontu had drunk out of sorrow, Giacobbe drank out of joy.

VIII

One morning towards the end of the summer, about three years after his conviction, Costantino awoke in a bad mood. The heat was oppressive and a sickening stench pervaded the room. One of the prisoners was snoring and bubbling like a saucepan on the boil.

Costantino had slept with Giovanna's last letter under his head. The letter was terse and very gloomy. It said that Giovanna and her mother were living in dire poverty and that the baby was seriously ill.

Costantino did not consider it cruel of her to write to him about these things. He wanted the truth, however unbearable, and it seemed to him that to share Giovanna's troubles and agonize because he could not help her was only his duty. A pointless duty, he knew, and this increased his anguish.

He had become a skilled shoemaker, and he worked swiftly, but he earned little, and all he earned – except that which the King of Spades took for his services – Costantino sent to Giovanna.

'You're a fool, I swear you are,' the ex-police inspector said to him. 'You need money for food. They ought to send you some of theirs.'

'They are so poor.'

'Are they? They have the sun. What more do they want? If you would eat and drink you'd be doing an act of charity. You're just a stick, my friend. Look at me now: I'm getting fatter. I live on air, but all the same I grow fat.'

He did indeed look like a little dumpling, but it was an unhealthy fatness, flabby and yellow. Costantino, on the other hand, was gaunt, with sunken eyes and almost transparent hands.

'The sun!' he thought bitterly. 'Oh, yes they have the sun! But what use is the sun when there's nothing to eat, when they're ill and suffering every kind of misery?'

He knew it was foolish of him but sometimes when he thought about his family he would cry like a baby.

Still he went on hoping. The years passed and the days fell away slowly and regularly, one after another, like drops of water in a cave, dripping from stone to stone. Almost all the convicts, particularly those with shorter sentences, were hoping for a pardon. They passed the time in calculating exactly the number of days that had gone by and the number still to go, and they never made a mistake. Some even counted the hours. Costantino thought it a foolish thing to do, smiling at the notion that he might either die or be set free before his sentence was up. It was all in God's hands. Costantino counted on being freed before he had served his time, but it passed so slowly, so slowly. That morning he felt it particularly, waking and feeling the warm paper of Giovanna's letter.

He arose and dressed, sighing. The man on his right stopped snoring, opened a bleary eye, and lay watching Costantino as if he did not recognize him. Then he shut his eye again and asked, 'Are you feeling poorly? Oh, yes, your son is ill. Why don't you tell the governor?'

'How can I tell the governor? He'd put me in solitary if he knew I received letters like this.'

'And on bread and chicken,' said another voice ironically. He meant bread and water.

Someone else laughed and his companions' indifference made Costantino feel utterly alone, lost in a burning waste.

He went to work anxiously awaiting the exercise hour, when he could speak to the King of Spades. That fat, yellow man, for whom he had no respect, was, nevertheless, indispensable to him. He was Costantino's only close friend. He alone understood, sympathized, helped. He demanded payment, it was true, but that in no way affected the position he occupied with many of the prisoners, especially his fellow countryman, who, in selfish despair, was already dreading the day when the King of Spades would have served his sentence and would have gone.

That morning a new prisoner made his appearance in the workshop. He was a northerner, tall and willowy with a wrinkled grey face and small pale eyes. It was difficult to tell how old he was, but the others laughed when he said he was twenty-two. He at once complained of the heat and of the smell of wax that thickened the air. He was no shoemaker. He was the only son of a rich wholesale shoe merchant – a gentleman, in short. He told them he had killed a rival in a love affair. Just that. The woman over whom he had committed the crime was dying of consumption and of grief. She was dying. Just that. The trouble was that the prisoner had a son by the sick woman. If she died, the child would be an orphan, a waif.

Costantino trembled, not because the prisoner's story moved him but because the baby and the woman reminded him of his Giovanna and Malthineddu.

The newcomer, who had begun to work quickly and skilfully, now stopped speaking and sat with bent head, intent on his work, his lower lip trembling like a child about to cry. Costantino watched him but just as the others ignored his grief, so he was now unable to share in the grief of others. The thought made him even sadder, even more desperate to get out.

As soon as he saw the King of Spades, Costantino drew him aside to a shady corner against the hot wall, but he found he could not speak of his suffering. Instead he told the man about the new prisoner.

The King of Spades shrugged his shoulders, then turned, spat against the wall, and said, 'If he wants to write too, tell him to be careful. There's someone sniffing around.'

'What are we going to do when you've gone?' asked Costantino sadly.

'You want me to stay here for ever, you rascal?'

'Good God, no! I wish you could get out tomorrow.'

The King of Spades sighed. His enemies, he said, were finding new ways of keeping him inside. He no longer expected a pardon, but the end of his term was at hand. Then he would go at once to the king and tell him everything. The king would order an instant reversal of the verdict and he himself, his innocence established, would be reinstated in his position and career. He promised everyone, especially Costantino, that he would get them a pardon. 'All will be well,' he announced, pleased with himself. He so enjoyed making promises that he came to believe in them himself.

'It may be tomorrow – who knows! It will be a good thing for everyone.'

'Good or bad,' said Costantino.

'Once I leave, perhaps you won't need me any more.' He immediately regretted his words, but seeing Costantino shake his head doubtfully, supposing that the King of Spades was referring to a pardon for him, the man looked at Costantino with genuine sympathy.

'But are you innocent, are you really innocent?' he asked. 'You can tell me everything now, dear friend. Do you remember that when I asked you the first time you said, "May I never see my son again if I am guilty"?'

'That's true. Now you're going to tell me that I may never see my son again. God may will it so, but I am innocent.'

The King of Spades turned to the wall and spat again. 'Be patient, my friend, be patient.' His voice was warm and sincere. He thought of himself as a superior man, for he set great store by his ability to recognize and respect honesty in others. This was how he had come, in his way, to love Costantino. He recognized a simple heart, made of metal so pure that not even the fearful corruption of the prison could taint it. It happened that he read the letters that passed through him to the prisoner. One day an anonymous letter had arrived, badly written and covered in smudges that looked like dead insects or little bugs. The letter said that Giovanna, the prisoner's wife, was allowing herself to be courted by Brontu Dejas, and that Bachisia, hoping for a divorce, wanted to go to Nuoro to present her daughter's case to a lawyer.

The ex-police inspector became angry, and his friend, the Delegate, who was still involved in his great work, heard him snorting and saw him puffing out his yellow cheeks. 'Stupid

Sardinian fools. What do they write to him for? There's nothing he can do except beat his head against the wall.'

The letter was not delivered and each time the King of Spades met the prisoner he gazed at him with profound sympathy, feeling at the same time pleased at his own goodness.

Three days later the child died, and Costantino received news of this at once. Hiding himself, he wept silently, putting on a good face to his cellmates. When the prisoner with the sick lover heard about the Sardinian's tragedy, he wept in a strange manner, like a squawking hen. His face, like that of an old, grey child, was so ludicrous when he wept that the man from Abruzzo, who had quarrelled with his brother, burst out laughing. His neighbour stuck an awl in his thigh, and he leapt up with a shout of pain but did not protest.

Costantino stared at his companion in bewilderment. Then he shook his head and went back to work. Silence fell and the Northerner calmed down. The low room was filled with the reflected glow from the courtyard, and the intense heat drew a pungent smell from the leather and from the prisoners' sweating hands and feet. The thirteen men in the workshop were under the continuous watch of a red-moustached warder, who looked like a sheepdog guarding a flock. Identically dressed, with shaven heads, and a slightly vacant expression on their faces, the prisoners all looked alike, as if they were brothers or relatives of some sort. But never as on that day had Costantino felt so out of sympathy, so apart from his companions in misfortune.

He stitched and stitched, hunched over, with a shoe resting between his knees on his leather apron. From time to time he inspected the shoe carefully, then he went back to sewing, tugging fiercely at the needle with both hands. Now that the baby was dead he had to work. Had he loved the child a lot? He did not know. Perhaps not much. He had only seen him once in Nuoro, through the iron bars of the visitors' room, crying in Giovanna's arms. The baby had a small red face, downy like a ripe apricot, and gleaming dark blue eyes like grape pips beneath his fringed cap. During the conversation he had cried and shrieked, terrified of the silent, impassive warders, and of those metal bars which he grabbed at with his little hands.

Costantino had no other memory of his Martino. As the years had gone by, he always imagined him red-faced and sobbing, his dark blue eyes hidden by the fringe of the red cap. He cast his mind into the future and saw Martino tall and slim, driving the cart, riding a horse, sowing and ploughing, a comfort and help to his mother. How the prisoner longed to return home! When sometimes he realized the hope was vain, his thoughts turned to his son. He loved the child more through his love for Giovanna than with the selfish affection that is born of habit and proximity.

Now the child was dead. The dream was dead. Let God's will be done. It was the thought of his wife's agony that caused Costantino the most grievous suffering. The King of Spades realized this when one day he spoke to the young man again in the hot shade of the wall. Instead of comforting Costantino, he said ironically, 'Well, my friend, don't drive yourself to desperation. You must think of it this way. If God, as you say, has called an innocent soul to himself, he has done it for the child's own good.'

'Why?' asked Costantino, his head bowed, arms limp, hands spread wide. 'Because he was poor?'

The King of Spades was in a philosophical mood, saying that far from being an evil, poverty may, on the contrary, some-times be a positive good. 'There are other evils, my friend. Think of yourself. Your wife will recover.'

'Oh, yes, she has the sun!' said Costantino, clenching his fists. 'The sun that scorches. Much use the sun is to her.'

'Pff,' puffed the other, inflating his fat, yellowish cheeks three times. Then staring thoughtfully at the nail on the little finger of his right hand he asked, 'Tell me, old fellow, what would you do if your wife were to take another husband?'

'Don't talk about such things today,' said Costantino in distress.

A silence followed.

'Look, my friend,' said the King of Spades, 'you don't follow what I mean. Your wife is honest enough, no doubt about that.

But she's young, and nature will take its course. While there's a child, a son, that's enough for her, for a young woman. But what if she's alone? What if she's tempted? You think not? What a naive fellow you are. Upon my word, you're so innocent, you're like a free man.'

Costantino raised his head. His sunken eyes opened round and wide, but suddenly they half-closed again.

'Giovanna wouldn't do that,' he said. 'She wouldn't do that,' he repeated to himself, but he felt as if a knife had touched his heart.

'Look,' the King of Spades went on, 'I don't believe she'd do it either. But tell me something, my friend. Now her son is dead, now she has no hopes for him or for you, wouldn't it be right for her to do it? She'd be a fool if she had the opportunity and didn't take it. If you are as good a Christian as you say, you'd let her do it.'

'If you don't shut up I'll strangle you,' said Costantino to himself. Then he thought of Brontu Dejas and repeated, more to convince himself than the other man, 'She'd never do that.'

'You're a fool, old fellow. If she did it, she'd be quite right. Believe me.'

'But I'm going back one day.'

'How does she know that?'

'I've been writing and telling her, and I'll go on telling her.'

The King of Spades wanted to laugh, but he restrained himself and after a short space he said, as if answering some inward question, 'It's all foolishness.'

'Yes,' replied Costantino, at once. But he could not stop thinking of Brontu Dejas, of the house with the portico, of the man's fields and flocks, and of Giovanna's poverty.

That night he wrote to comfort her, repeating that he still hoped for divine mercy. 'Perhaps God wanted to test us further, taking from us the fruit we conceived in sin. His will be done. Now, more than ever, I have a feeling that the day of my deliverance is near.'

For a long time he pondered, wondering whether to mention the horrible things hinted at by the ex-police inspector. But no. He thought he was being shrewd by not exciting her interest. When he had written the letter he grew calmer, but an inexorable jealousy began to devour his mind, and from that day forth the King of Spades, with brutal pity, continued to inject the terrible poison into his blood.

'He has to get used to it,' thought Burrai. 'Otherwise the poor, simple fellow will die of a broken heart.'

'Dear, dear fellow,' he blustered one day in October. 'You know nothing about women. Empty vessels, nothing else. I was engaged once. I suppose that seems impossible to you? She deceived me – even before we were married. But your wife's in quite a different situation: she's poor and she's young. Has she blood in her veins or not? If Dejas wants to marry her, she'd be a goose not to take him.'

'Who's Dejas? Who told you about him?' asked Costantino in surprise.

'Didn't you tell me yourself?'

Costantino was sure he had never mentioned the man. But his mind was so confused sometimes. Oh God, oh good San Costantino. How had he come to speak of it?

'Well yes,' he admitted. 'I'm afraid of him. He courted her, he wanted to marry her. But he's a drunkard, he's dull as mud. She'd never do a terrible thing like that. Let's talk about something else, please.'

They did, still speaking in dialect so that the other prisoners would not understand. They talked of the consumptive student who was growing ever closer to the gates of the other world; they talked of the Delegate, who spoke aloud to himself, praising his own work; they talked of the magpie, which had grown thin and was shedding its plumage in old age.

Gossip, hatred, resentment, loves, slander, united and incited the prisoners. Costantino stayed immune to it all. He, the student, and the Delegate seemed to live apart from the others, speaking only to the ex-police inspector, who was the focal point of almost all the secrets in the prison and who remained above them all, indispensable to everyone.

Many envied the intimacy that he accorded Costantino and begged the young prisoner to intercede for them to the King of Spades for certain favours. They offered Costantino money, and he was tempted to take it, so desperate was he to support Giovanna as much as possible. He could think of nothing else. The constant hinting by the King of Spades pricked like a thorn and became ever more hateful to him. One day they had a serious argument and for some time afterwards did not even exchange a greeting. Costantino felt he was suffocating. He felt as if he was cut off for ever from the outside world, and he was the first to climb down and make peace.

Autumn drew on. The air became cooler, the sky seemed made of blue velvet – soft, distant, gentle as a dream. Sometimes the wind bore the scent of ripe fruit.

Costantino felt less depressed, but full of melancholy. In order to send money to Giovanna he deprived himself of everything and grew anaemic. While the other prisoners received a little money, he deprived himself even of what he earned.

'I don't understand,' said the ex-police inspector. 'You seem to be getting younger and healthier, and yet you are almost transparent.'

Costantino's face burned and the blood sang in his ears. He felt more homesick than he had been in the first year. He saw the great high plain drowsing in the autumnal calm, yellow beneath the clear sky, and the mountains warmed by the gentle sun. He smelled the fragrance of the vines and the fruit which ripened late in that land of shepherds and bees. He saw the foxes, the hares, the hives, the wild birds, the horses, the hedgerows laden with blackberries – all the things that had cheered his unhappy childhood. Remembering his uncle, the cruel old Vulture, who had tormented him during his life and now, after his death, was tormenting him again, he felt a surge of hatred. Then he thought, 'Now he is no more,' and he repented and prayed for the man's soul.

He did not hate the real murderer nor Brontu Dejas, who as yet had given him no cause for complaint, nor the King of Spades, who continually tormented him. He had not the strength to hate. He felt a gentle melancholy in his blood, as if he were on the verge of sleep, and a feeling of love, tender and sad as the autumn sun. He thought of Giovanna constantly.

The more the time passed, the more he felt he loved her. She was his distant homeland, his family, freedom, life. In her was all hope, faith, strength, serenity, the joy of living. She was his soul. To keep Giovanna he would have remained forty years in prison. At the same time he longed for liberty just because he did not want to lose her.

That winter he suffered badly from the cold. His face, even his fingernails, grew waxen. During the exercise hour when he went out into the sun, his teeth chattered like those of an old man. He was always asking to go to confession, and he told the young chaplain of his fears.

'Who put that idea into your head?' asked the confessor, his black eyes glinting.

'A fellow countryman of mine, ex-police inspector Burrai, the King of Spades.'

'May God bless and protect you,' murmured the chaplain, becoming thoughtful. He knew the King of Spades well. He then tried to console the prisoner, asking if Giovanna was still writing to him. Giovanna now wrote very seldom. After the child's death she seemed to have nothing more to say. The last thing she had written was that the weather was very cold. It snowed continually. A man had frozen to death crossing the mountains. There was terrible hunger in the village.

Costantino found all this unbearable. Often he dreamed he was to be taken to Nuoro and freed. From there he was trying to walk to his own village. He was cold, he could go no further, he was dying, dying. He awoke frozen, agony clutching at his heart.

'You are very weak, dear brother,' said the confessor. 'It is weakness that makes you think these ugly thoughts. Your wife is a good Christian. She'd never do you any wrong. Go away now. Put these notions out of your mind. You must build up your health. Eat, drink something. Are you earning any money?'

'A little, and I send all of it to my wife. She is so poor. Oh, I eat enough. No, I'm not weak. I don't like to drink, it makes me sick.'

'Well, calm down. I'll have a word with Burrai.'

He spoke to the King of Spades, and accused him of putting gloomy ideas into Ledda's head.

'He is a poor, half-starved boy, leave him in peace or he'll get seriously ill.'

The King of Spades looked at the priest for a while out of his shrewd little pig-eyes. At last he shook his head and said, 'I'm doing it for his own good.'

'Come off it!'

'Listen to me, my friend. This winter there's little to fear as far as the young woman's concerned, because it's damned cold. I imagine it's only the old woman, Costantino's mother-in-law, who's working on the girl, advising her to take advantage of the situation. But when spring comes, then just you watch out. Mark my words.'

The chaplain made a long face and began to protest. The other man watched him, his small eyes full of malice, and then he explained the situation clearly, describing the mother-in-law's greed, the wife's youth, the dangers of spring. The chaplain became angry.

'You're intolerable!' he said. 'Why are you making these things up? Why are you tormenting that poor boy? Just because the woman had a suitor when she was a girl, it doesn't have to mean . . .'

'Calm down and look at this,' said the King of Spades, showing him the anonymous letter from Costantino's village.

The chaplain saw the matter was very serious. He asked the ex-policeman to leave the letter with him, saying, 'Do you take money from Ledda?'

'Of course, just a little bit. Isn't that fair? Aren't I risking being put in solitary by helping him?'

'And do you think that it is your duty to do what you're doing?'

'What's duty? Helping the next man is our duty, and that's what I do.'

The chaplain was rereading the letter closely.

'When I'm free,' went on Burrai, 'if those influential people whom I have at my disposal don't have me reappointed to my post, I shall make it my profession to circulate all the secret correspondence of all prisoners in Italy. A sort of agency.'

'You'll be back here soon.'

'Ho. I'll do it as a duty. A secret agency, my dear friend. What about that?'

'Thank you,' said the other man, folding up the letter. 'Why are you flattering the poor wretch like this with your attentions?'

'Thank you,' replied Burrai coldly. 'Isn't your job – comforting people – an illusion too? Isn't it a kind act? If we don't have any hope what *do* we have?'

'Then,' said the chaplain in a pleasant voice, 'do me the favour of tormenting someone other than this poor boy. Give him some hope, or he's going to become ill.'

The ex-police inspector promised grudgingly. 'He'll die of the shock,' he thought. 'We'll see in the spring. We'll see whether I'm right or not.'

When they met, Costantino smiled at him and asked him if he had seen the priest, as they called the chaplain amongst themselves, and what he had said. Burrai was leaning against the dark damp wall, his hands behind his back, and in dialect, under his breath, he cursed long and quietly against no one in particular.

'Who do you mean?' asked Costantino. 'Who are you angry with?'

'No one. Yes, I saw the priest, he gave me a telling off as if I was a child. He's a child himself! A piglet with yellow, rancid fat. Do you know, I read that in Russia rancid bacon is in great demand?'

'What did he tell you?'

'What did he tell me? He said . . . I don't remember now. Oh, yes, he told me that thing we were talking about is just a fantasy of mine. It seems I have a rich imagination. Forgive me, dear friend. Your wife will never betray you – as true as I stand here.'

Costantino watched him eagerly. The man was not joking, he never joked. He was telling the truth.

'Ah, he scolded you for it then. I'm glad.'

75

'This wall,' said the King of Spades, straightening up and looking at his hands that were red and pitted with the pressure of his having leaned on them, 'look, my friend, this wall is like chocolate. It's hot and sticky. If only it were chocolate it would be doubly good. We could eat our way through it and escape. Have you ever eaten chocolate?'

'Of course! Giovanna liked it. But it's so expensive.'

'Oh, you get on my nerves,' cried the other man. 'Yes, she'll wait for you for another twenty-three years, have no fear.'

'No, I'll get out before then. Anyway, aren't you going to the king to get me a pardon?'

'Yes, from the king himself. You don't believe me, do you? I'm going to the king. He receives all the officials, and am I not an official?' And he laughed.

After that, Costantino always brought the conversation around to the same subject. The other man veered away from it whenever he could, and he ceased tormenting Costantino about it. One day around this time Costantino found that five lire had been deposited in his account.

'It's from him, it's from him,' he exclaimed. 'It's from the priest. What a good man he is! But I don't want it.'

'Don't be foolish,' said the King of Spades. 'Take it, or he'll be insulted. "I don't want it." Is that how you thank someone?'

'But I'm ashamed. And what can I do with it, anyway?'

'Eat, drink. You need it, believe me. I suppose you want to send it over there. To hell with you! If you're that stupid I'll spit in your face. She doesn't even write any more.'

'What's there to write to me about?' said Costantino, trying to reassure himself. 'She'll get work now that winter's over.'

'Yes, it's over! And spring is on its way,' said the other man meaningfully. 'Now you'll see. When does the warm weather come to your village? At home it's hot by March.'

'Not until June with us. It's so beautiful there then. The grass grows high, high. The flocks are shorn, the bees make their honey.'

'What an idyll. You don't know what an idyll means? Well, it means . . . to hell with it. Let's wait for June. Is it a long time since you last went to confession?'

'Yes. Two weeks.'

'A long time. Oh, what a fool you are, my friend. I've never been to confession. My conscience is clear as a mirror. Look,' he pointed at the student, whose face was waxy and his shaven head so white it looked as if it were powdered, 'he's the one who really needs confession. He is knocking at the door of eternity.'

Only shortly after, in fact, the student was taken to the infirmary, where he died at the end of March. The man with the consumptive lover kept an anxious eye on the sick man's progress, and when the student died he wept like a child for a whole day. He wept not only for the poor dead man, but also for his own sick sweetheart. The student's death cast a strange melancholy over the King of Spades. He began to philosophize on life and death, and he embarked on long discussions with the Delegate. In Costantino's company, Burrai lost himself in nostalgic memories of his distant homeland.

'Once I went through your village, or near it,' he said. 'I don't know exactly. There was a wood of cork oaks, rock-roses and wild strawberry trees. Over these trees it looked as if it had rained blood. The scent was so strong it was like tobacco. There's a cross on top of a rock. You can see the sea in the distance.'

'That's Cherbomine Wood. I know it so well. Once on a rock, a huntsman saw a stag with a golden horn. He shot and killed it. As it lay dying, the stag gave a human cry and said, "My penance is over." They say in its body was the soul of a man who had committed a serious crime. They put the cross there.'

'And the horn, my friend?'

'They say when the huntsman drew close, he saw that the horn was an ordinary antler.'

'Pff! How stupid you peasants are! Oh, look, spring is coming,' said the King of Spades, looking at the sky. 'Spring excites me. I used to hunt in the marshy lagoons near Cagliari. Oh, those lagoons. They are like scattered fragments of a looking-glass. Purple lilies grow around them. Flamingoes fly overhead in long skeins, so beautiful you can't bear to watch them. I closed one eye. Bang! Down came a flamingo. The others flew on by, silently, in a line. I hurled myself into the middle of the pond to pick up the flamingo. It was quick and slippery as a fish. I was eighteen years old.'

'What did you do with the flamingo?'

'I stuffed it. They have long legs, soft as velvet. Have you seen those marshes? Oh, yes, of course, you were in the mines near Cagliari. I shall go back there to die in peace.'

'You're sad today.'

'Why not, dear friend? It's spring. It's sad to spend Easter in prison. This year I'm going to do the Easter observances.'

'I've already done them.'

'Ah, have you now?'

The two prisoners fell silent, lost in reminiscences.

April, May, and June went by. The dreary prison walls once again became ovens. Tormenting mosquitoes awoke. Sickly smells began once more to pollute the air. In the cobblers' workshop, under the watchful eye of the red-faced warder, the leather, the wax, and the sweat exuded an intolerable smell.

Now weaker than ever, Costantino suffered terribly from the insects. In previous years he had slept deeply, ignoring the bites. But now he slept lightly and sharp pains that were not always caused by the insects awoke him with a start, making his whole body tremble. Then insomnia began – or a half-stupor worse than insomnia – that merged into nightmare. He tossed and turned, suffocated by the heat. Often the orange light of dawn arrived before he could close his eyes. Then he would be overcome by a great exhaustion, an unconquerable urge to sleep, and it would be time to get up.

At the end of May, Giovanna wrote begging him not to send any more money. They earned enough to live modestly. She did not write again. Still he did not doubt her faithfulness. The last letter even seemed to him to be proof of affection. The King of Spades waited for him every day with a certain anxiety. He would fix Costantino with a piercing eye and ask solicitously, 'Any news?' And if Costantino wondered at this question the police inspector also wondered, not saying what about. He only observed, 'It's hot.'

'Yes, it's hot.'

'Spring's over.'

'I should say so.'

'Let's hope the famine is over in your village.'

'It must be over. My wife doesn't want me to send her any more money.'

'Ah. I know what you mean, my friend.'

The ex-police inspector did not know what to think; he became almost angry at finding his prophecy was not coming true.

One day Costantino did not come to the exercise hour. Burrai found out that his countryman was in the infirmary. A strange fear gripped him and to the old magpie that fluttered around calling in a nasal voice, 'Costanti, Costanti,' he replied, 'Costantino has been struck by a thunderbolt.'

All the prisoners crowded around, curious to know something. But he held up his hands as if to keep them away. 'I don't know anything. Leave me alone.'

'He finished at nine o'clock,' said one of them. 'Costantino was working at the cobblers' bench. Then a warder came to fetch him. He got up at once, wide-eyed and pale and trembling, and he went away with the warder. He didn't come back.'

Costantino never forgot that day. It was a hot, overcast morning. The clouds seemed to weigh upon the cobblers' workshop, sending heavy shadows halfway up the walls. The prisoners, the leather of their aprons stinking, were in a bad mood.

One of them, who was in constant fear of death, related that in his village, at dead of night, long white watery phantoms were seen running into the river, and he asked a companion whether he had ever seen such a thing.

'Not I! I don't believe in such nonsense.'

'You call it nonsense,' muttered the other in a dull, toneless voice, his eyes fixed on his work.

'Mutton head,' someone else said under his breath.

The first man grew angry. 'Can't I talk to myself?' the other protested: 'Can't I say mutton head, calf head, dog head? What's it to you? Can't I talk to the shoes?'

It was at that point that the warder had come and called for

Costantino. Costantino had spent a sleepless night. He had opened his eyes wide, got up quickly, and his face blanched. He thought he was dreaming.

'Who wants me?' he had asked, following the warder.

He was led into a dirty room lined with shelves heaped with dusty papers. The grimy windows were closed. Behind the windows was a red grating and behind that could be seen the cloudy sky which seemed, in its turn, covered with dust. In the room, behind a high, dusty desk, a man sat writing. Some letters lay in front of him. He was almost invisible among the dust and the papers. When the prisoner came in he raised his head, showing a flushed face with a small chin entirely covered by a drooping blond moustache. His large milky blue eyes rested on Costantino without apparently seeing him, for he began to write again rapidly.

Costantino, who had met the man before, remained standing, his heart thumping. In his nervousness he thought of the story of the ghost in the river, the prisoner who had said 'mutton head', and he wondered if the other man were right to be offended. The only sound in the room was the scratch of the pen on the coarse paper. The round, dull eyes fixed on him again. Costantino shivered, glanced nervously round, and waited. 'Perhaps they've found out that I am innocent,' he thought with a surge of joy.

The man had begun to write again. Then, in a deep voice, he called, 'What's your name?'

'Costantino Ledda.'

'From where?'

'Orlei, in Sardinia – Province of Sassari.'

'Very good.'

Silence. The man went on writing. Suddenly he cleared his throat loudly, looked up, and at last seemed to see the prisoner. Costantino lowered his eyes.

'Very good. Are you married?'

'Yes.'

'Children?'

'We had one, but he died.'

'You were married by civil ceremony only?'

'Yes,' replied Costantino, raising terrified eyes. On the man's fat, pink hand could be seen a ring with a purple stone, and between the finger and thumb the tip of a black pen. Not knowing where to look, in his bewilderment, Costantino fixed his eyes on the pen. He felt as if he were in a dream, where a terrible disaster impended.

'Why did you not have a religious ceremony?' the man went on.

'Because we were poor, and we needed money for the wedding feast. When finally we had enough, the disaster happened, on the very eve of the wedding. Now I'm waiting until I'm set free. I'm still waiting. We could have the wedding even with me inside here, but it's better to wait.'

Even without glancing at his torturer, he thought he detected a smile in the man's eyes.

'Well,' said the torturer, 'we have a letter from your mayor, who has taken on the task of informing you, on behalf of your wife, and in anticipation of the divorce law, that she intends to contract a religious marriage with a certain Brontu Dejas. What do you want to do about it? Why – what's the matter?'

Costantino slid to the ground like a rag doll.

IX

In the Porru house, in the guest room, Giovanna was sorting out some materials bought that day in Nuoro. She was plumper and had lost a little of her girlish air, but she was still beautiful.

She was inspecting the linens and cottons closely, turning them over and feeling them with a preoccupied air, as if unsatisfied with the choice she had made. Then she folded them carefully, wrapped them in paper, and placed them in a saddlebag. She was preparing her trousseau. Having obtained legal separation from Costantino, Giovanna had agreed to marry Brontu, who had promised to find a way of marrying her in a church.

Giovanna and her mother had come to Nuoro for the specific purpose of retaining the lawyer Porru in the ensuing divorce case, and to do some shopping. They had borrowed the money, secretly, from Anna-Rosa Dejas, Giacobbe's sister, a lady who was fond of Giovanna because she had helped Bachisia out as the girl's foster-mother.

It was the dead of winter. But the two women had courageously undertaken the hardships of the journey to come to Nuoro to lay in a stock of linen, cottons, kerchieves and woollen materials.

The wedding was to take place even more discreetly than the marriage of a widow but it did not matter. Bachisia wanted her daughter to go to her new home fully provided for, like a young bride from a good family.

The village was buzzing with gossip about the scandalous event. Giacobbe Dejas, Isidoro Pane, and other friends no longer spoke to the Era women. Giacobbe had howled like a dog, threatening, begging, but Bachisia had thrown him out of the house.

Although her son had supported the separation case, Porredda too received the friends coldly in Nuoro – not that this lessened Giovanna's preoccupation with her purchases. It seemed she had been slightly swindled over the linen, and the woollen kerchief with its large crimson roses had too short a fringe. There was a stain on one ribbon. All this was very worrying.

Evening fell, as on that other occasion, but everything around her – the weather, her heart – was different. The guest room now had a fine window through whose panes came the brief, cold winter twilight. The new furniture, still smelling of varnish, shone with a pale gleam. The door opened on to a covered terrace and a new granite staircase led down into the old courtyard. The whole house had been renovated. The 'Doctor' had gone into the legal business. He was as much sought after for civil cases as for criminal ones. The most vile and desperate criminals, everyone who feared the law most, entrusted themselves to him.

Giovanna finished folding and repacking the linen. The saddlebag was stuffed full on both sides, and the young woman lifted it up and shook it so that the packages might slip down to the bottom. Then she stood frowning thoughtfully. She went out and slowly descended the stairs, pushing her hands into the two short slits in the front of her woollen skirt.

The January night was clear, but cold. On a sky of vitreous blue a few silver stars trembled with cold. Crossing the courtyard, Giovanna saw behind the lighted windows of the dining-room Grazia's white face and glowing eyes. The girl was holding a fashion magazine in her hand. She had become tall and beautiful, and she always dressed in the latest fashion. When she saw the guest she greeted her with a smile, but made no move. Giovanna went into the kitchen. It too had been renovated with white walls, shining brick ovens, and an oil lamp that hung from the vaulted ceiling.

Bachisia's little green eyes, staring out of her yellow,

hawklike face, could not get enough of it. She had not changed at all. She sat beside the fire with the servant, a dirty ragged wench who laughed loudly, showing jutting teeth. Porredda cooked, scolding the maid for the way she laughed. So, the mistress does the cooking while the maid sits by the fire and laughs, does she? What did she mean by it? The good woman could not stand idle for a moment even though she was now the mother of a distinguished lawyer.

Giovanna sat down at a distance from the fire, her hands still in the slits of her skirt.

'Look!' said Bachisia to her daughter in an envious voice. 'This kitchen is like a front parlour. You must furnish your kitchen like this.'

'Yes, yes,' replied the girl absently.

'Of course you must. Old mother-in-law Martina is a miser, but you must make her understand that money is made to be spent. Look at this kitchen. It's a paradise. This is the life.'

'Maybe the mistress doesn't want to spend anything.' Giovanna shrugged. 'It's her money.'

The maid laughed again, but Porredda, who did not want to get involved in her guests' conversation, turned round sharply and ordered the girl to grate the cheese for the macaroni.

'What's the matter?' Bachisia asked her daughter. 'Why these sighs?'

'She's remembering. How could she possibly not remember? After all she's a human being, not an animal,' thought Porredda.

Giovanna spoke angrily. 'They've cheated us, I tell you. The linen isn't any good. The cloth is stained. A bad stain.'

'Mercy me!' exclaimed the servant, imitating Bachisia's voice, as she grated the cheese.

Then Porredda vented all her rage on the wench, all the horror that the guests aroused in her. She called her the names she wanted to call Giovanna – shameless, vile, wretched, ungrateful – and she threatened to beat the girl with the ladle. In her fear, the maid scraped her finger and held it up, bleeding. Just then the young lawyer limped in, wrapped in a voluminous overcoat that looked like a cloak with sleeves. His chubby pink face looked as contented as a nursing baby's.

He asked what there was to eat, then he deigned to sit next to Bachisia, and chatted with her until dinner-time. Efes Maria came in wanting dinner at once. In the dining-room, two old sideboards of yellow wood gleamed, and the flagstones on the floor, the stove, the flower vases, gave the place the gracious air of a gentleman's room. Efes Maria looked about him with an air of satisfaction, while Porredda moved round uncomfortably, her big feet in shoes like flat-irons.

Just as on that long past evening, she came in carrying the steaming macaroni, and everyone sat down at the table. Bachisia sat beside young Grazia marvelling at her dress with its wide lace sleeves, like wings.

'I've never seen those where we come from. There are no ladies at home. You ladies here are all like angels.'

'Or bats,' said Efes Maria. 'These fashions! When I was a boy, the gentry were big and solid. They were like houses. There aren't many ladies and gentlemen around nowadays. The mayor's wife, the ladies – '

'What about those things they used to wear behind them,' said Porredda. 'I remember, they were like saddles. Don't you believe me?'

'The last time I came,' said Bachisia, 'these wings were tiny. Now they've grown up. They're still growing.'

Grazia went on eating, paying no attention. The doctor was also eating greedily, watching his nephew, who was smiling like a cherub.

'They're growing up,' the doctor said. 'Soon they'll spread their wings.'

Grazia shrugged her shoulders and neither replied nor raised her eyes. She found her young uncle intolerable these days. He had been her first love – a crush – but now she sometimes found him ridiculous.

The all chatted while from time to time Porredda got up from the table, went out, and came back. Now and again the conversation would die away and an almost embarrassed silence ensued. As on that other occasion, they tried to avoid the subject that most concerned the guests, who did not object at all. But it was Bachisia herself who unintentionally brought

85

up the topic when she asked whether it were true, as everyone claimed, that the doctor was to marry his niece.

The Porrus looked at each other and laughed softly. Paolo looked at the girl and said with not the most cheerful irony. 'What? No. She's to marry the distinguished sub-prefect.'

Grazia raised and then quickly lowered her face. Her eyes smouldered and she blushed.

'He's old,' said Minnia. 'I know him. He always walks past the station. Ugh! He has a long red beard. And a top hat.'

'A top hat too?'

'Yes, a top hat. He's a widower.'

'Shut up, you,' said Grazia quickly, turning on her sister.

'I won't shut up. He's a Freemason too. He won't baptize the children. He won't get married in church. Isn't it true? He won't marry in church.'

'The young lady is well-informed,' said Efes Maria, polite as ever.

Porredda, who was listening closely, and who was barely able to restrain a scream at the word 'freemason', raised her hands in the air and broke in:

'Yes, he's a Mason – one of those people who pray to the devil. My niece wants to take him because he's rich. We're all damned. Grazia reads bad books, filthy newspapers, and doesn't want to go to confession. Oh, those censored books! I can't sleep thinking about them. Then there's Paolo, who has studied on the mainland, where they don't believe in God any longer. It's not right, but it's understandable because the two of them don't believe in God any more. But we know nothing of books. We have never been on a train – that devil's horse – why don't we believe in God any more, in our good Lord who died for us on the cross? Why, I ask, why? Because you, Giovanna Era, you're marrying another man, when you already have a husband.'

Grazia, who was smiling at her grandmother's invective, lifted a grave face at these last words. Paolo, pushing his knife through the prongs of his fork and smiling at his mother's words, made a sudden gesture, and Efes Maria, his face arranged in a mask of tragedy, looked spitefully at Giovanna.

Giovanna blushed but said cynically, 'I'm not married any longer, Porredda. Ask your son.'

'I've no son. That's the devil's son,' said the woman scornfully.

It seemed almost as if Giovanna were blaming Paolo for what she was about to do, because he had supported the separation case, and was promising an immediate divorce.

Then they all laughed at Porredda's anger, every one of them, including Minnia, including the maid who came in carrying a plate of cheese. In spite of her anger, Porredda took the plate and passed it courteously to Bachisia.

'My friend,' said the old woman sadly, 'you are so generous, but you are well-off. Your husband is as strong as a tower, you are surrounded by a crown of stars, look at them. If you knew what poverty was and the thought of begging in old age. Do you understand? In old age.'

'Bravo!' cried Paolo.

'That's not what matters, Bachisia Era,' replied Porredda. 'The reason you do not trust divine providence is because you don't believe in God. How do you know whether you'll be a beggar or a rich woman? Won't Costantino Ledda come back?'

'He'll be a beggar too,' said Bachisia coldly.

'God knows whether he'll return,' remarked the lawyer brutally. It was known that Costantino was ill with consumption.

To appear upset, as she may indeed have been, Giovanna hid her face in her hands.

'Anyway the real marriage is the religious one,' she muttered. 'If God has punished us it's as Costantino himself said – because we were married outside God's law.'

'You tell him that when he comes back,' cried Porredda. 'Paolo himself said that for the time being you can't marry another man. If Costantino comes back he'll kill you or have you put in prison.'

'That will be my punishment,' murmured Giovanna resignedly. 'No one can escape their fate.'

'You know what I've told you dozens of times,' said Paolo. 'This is all nonsense. Take Brontu if you like him, but don't marry him. Then if Costantino returns and you are tired of

Brontu, you can take Costantino again. Man and woman should be united spontaneously, and separate when they don't get on. Man – '

'You're an animal,' screamed Porredda, though it was not the first time she had heard her son speak in this way. 'It's the end of the world, the Day of Judgement. God is tired, and with good cause. He'll send the flood to punish us. I've already heard there's been an earthquake.'

'Earthquakes are always happening,' remarked Efes Maria, who didn't know whether to take his wife's side or his son's. Perhaps at heart he was on his wife's side, but he did not want to lose his educated son's esteem by showing it.

Paolo was silent, regretting what he had said. He was too fond of his mother to want to anger her pointlessly. Giovanna took her hands from her face and spoke with gentle humility. 'God, who sees the circumstances of our lives, will not be offended.'

'But he himself has punished you,' said Porredda.

'That's to be seen,' shouted Bachisia, who was beginning to spit out venom. 'Doesn't it mean, on the contrary, that Giovanna's and my punishment is finished if God is giving her the chance to marry a young man who loves her, who can make her forget all her suffering?'

'He's rich too,' observed Efes Maria. They did not know whether he was serious or joking.

Giovanna had lost the thread of the conversation, but she tried to conclude it in a sweet, humble voice. 'Dear Porredda. You can't know. God sees into our hearts. He will forgive me. Costantino is as if dead. Elias Portolu, the priest from our village – he's a good man, he's one of us, do you know him? He speaks like a saint and never gets angry. Even he said that only death can release you from marriage. He said, go and be blessed then, if you do not know what is right. We have to live, don't we? What if you have nothing to live on, no work, nothing, nothing at all? Tell me, Porredda, what if I had been another woman? Well, what would have happened? Then it would really have been mortal sin.'

'Mortal sin and then old age spent in poverty,' repeated Bachisia.

The maid brought the fruit, black gleaming grapes and wrinkled yellow pears like autumn leaves. The old mistress of the house took the basket of fruit to the old guest and watched her with compassion. All Porredda's anger, her contempt, her scorn fell away before the frailty of these two women. She said to herself, 'Good St Francis, forgive them because they are ignorant. They are wild and primitive.' Then she spoke in a gentler voice. 'We are old, Bachisia Era, and you too will become old, Giovanna Era. Tell me something now. What happens after old age?'

'Death.'

'Death. Death certainly. And what is after death?'

'Eternity,' said Paolo laughing, eating grapes like a greedy boy, bringing the fruit up to his mouth and tearing out the pips with his teeth.

'Eternity. Of course it's eternity. What do you say, Giovanna Era, is it eternity or not? Bachisia, yes or no?'

'It is,' answered the guests.

'It is, but you're not thinking of eternity.'

'It's pointless to think,' said Paolo, getting up. He had spent too much time with these two women, who only interested him because they still had to pay him.

'I must go. People are waiting for me at my office. I'll see you soon. You aren't leaving yet?'

'Tomorrow morning at dawn.'

He went off, and after him Grazia also left the room, having not spoken at all during dinner, and Efes Maria sat astride the chair and began to read the *New Sardinia*. Among the three women, who were each eating a pear, a grave silence reigned. There was a heavy weight pressing on them. With her primitive intuition, Porredda saw that the souls of the wild guests and the souls of her civilized descendants were bitten by the same evil – the greed for money.

X

The following day, just as on that long gone morning, Giovanna was the first to get up. The winter dawn, cold but sparkling, paled behind the curtained windows. Giovanna, who had gone to sleep in a sad mood, more hardened than upset by Porredda's remarks, looked at the window and felt happy. She saw it was going to be a fine day and therefore a good journey.

Her thoughts as she lay in bed the previous evening had wandered from Costantino to eternity to her dead baby and to many melancholy things.

'I'm not really bad,' she had said to herself. 'God can see what is in our hearts and he judges intentions more than actions. I loved Costantino and I wept buckets of tears. Now I have no tears left. I don't think he'll ever come back or, if he does, it'll be when we're old and cannot weep any more. Meanwhile I'm flesh and blood like other women. I'm poor and it's hard for me to resist temptation and sin. To escape one or the other I must take the place God has assigned me. Yes, Porredda, I am thinking of eternity, and it's to save my soul that I'm doing what I'm doing. No, I'm not wicked, not really wicked.'

Bit by bit she had comforted herself with the thought that she was, at heart, good and generous. If in the depths of her conscience – from whence arose the feeling of sadness that engulfed her – she did not really think that way, at least her mind told her she was right. Thus comforted she had fallen asleep.

Now the clear bright dawn was beating against the windows of the guest room, and Giovanna thought of the sun and became cheerful again.

Her mother awoke too and at once looked out of the window. 'It's going to be a fine day,' she said, pleased.

They got up. Porredda was already in the kitchen. Polite and solicitous, she served coffee to the guests and helped them saddle their horse. She seemed to have forgotten the previous evening's conversation, but as soon as the two women had left she made a little sign of the cross in the air. She felt as if mortal sin travelled with them.

'Until we meet again. God be with you on your journey,' she said, closing the door.

This time the Era women were travelling alone. They descended into the valley, crossed the bottom, climbed up the other side to the mountains whose peaks, covered with glittering white snow, were sketched harshly on the horizon.

It was cold. There was no wind, but the air was piercing and, heightened by the continuous noise of rushing streams, an indescribable silence reigned over the great wild valley. Short, vivid green winter grass, sprinkled with hoar-frost, covered the verges of the twisting brown paths. The moss on the rocks smelled rank. A wild, fresh cold rejuvenated the valleys from which an occasional gnarled, bare tree rose up suddenly like a naked hermit, exposed as a penance to the cold and the dawn light. On the cultivated land the earth was black, and low moss-covered walls climbed and dropped down, twisting like huge green worms.

On and on went the two women, their hands, faces, and feet frozen. They forded the stream at a wide place where the water flowed shallow and silent. Then they came out of the valley and began to climb the mountain. The sun peered over the horizon, bright but cold, and the mountains looked blue against a golden sky. The wind blew through stunted scrub, carrying with it a smell of damp rocks.

Bachisia thought of the greedy satisfaction Martina would feel when she saw Giovanna's trousseau. Giovanna thought of Brontu and of the strange things he said when he was drunk. When the church of St Francis came in sight, white in the sun, on the slope of a hill among frost-covered scrub, they thought of Costantino and said an *Ave Maria* for him. They reached home shortly after midday. Flanked by damp fields, under the frozen breath of the great snow-swathed sphinxes, Orlei was colder than Nuoro, and here the sun scarcely managed to warm the grass in the damp alleyways. The roofs were rusty with lichen and some were overgrown with vegetation. Dampness darkened the walls and the cold gave a reddish tinge to the bare trees. Purple smoke spiralled up into the infinite solitude of the clear sky. As usual the little village was quiet and as if deserted. On the walls, pennywort opened its green, fleshy calyces, while speckled lizards warmed themselves in the sun and snails and gleaming beetles crawled from stone to stone.

Beneath the portico, at a point where the sun shone through, Martina sat spinning. Seeing her two neighbours return she was overcome by an urge to learn what they had packed in the saddlebag, but she did not move and replied only stiffly to their greeting.

Towards evening Brontu returned from the fields. He visited his betrothed every third day, and on this occasion his mother accompanied him, eager to know what the Eras had brought from Nuoro.

A meagre fire of juniper wood burned in Bachisia's hearth, throwing long beams of reddish light on the floor and the brick walls of the kitchen. Giovanna wanted to light the candle, but the Dejas prevented her – Martina out of instinctive meanness and Brontu because in the half-dark he could watch his betrothed all the better.

Giovanna's behaviour before her future mother-in-law and Brontu was very strange. She became tender, gentle and, in a soft girlish voice, she made wise observations. She lowered her long eyelashes, making herself as demure as a fifteen-year-old girl, acting not out of guile but by instinct. Brontu was madly in love with her, so much so that when he was drunk he would run away from her, kneel down, and sing hymns half-remembered from his boyhood. Then he would weep with remorse at his drunkenness and swear never to touch a drop again in his whole life.

That evening he was perfectly sober, and he spoke calmly,

casting Giovanna long passionate looks. He smiled and his teeth gleamed in the fire's reflection.

Bachisia told the Dejas about the journey, describing the lawyer, the wings worn by the ladies, the Porru kitchen, but she did not mention the conversation they had had with Porredda, nor the things they had bought, for she knew Martina was dying to see them. She herself was dying to show off all the finery.

'What about you, Giovanna?' asked Brontu, poking the fire with a stick. 'You're thoughtful tonight. What's the matter?'

'I'm tired,' she replied, and asked suddenly for news of Giacobbe Dejas.

'That madman? He goes on pestering me. I'll end up by kicking him. He doesn't need to work for me any more.'

'I don't know,' said Bachisia. 'He used to be a happy man. Now he has a house, dammit, and they say he is going to get married, but he has such a temper. You know he wanted to beat us.'

'Hasn't he ever been back?'

'Never.'

'Isidoro Pane neither,' said Giovanna in a low voice.

'I thought I saw him go by here yesterday,' remarked Martina.

Giovanna raised her head quickly, but she did not speak and Brontu exclaimed laughing, 'You don't need his leeches.'

'Well,' asked Martina, after a short silence, 'haven't you brought me a present from Nuoro? You're making me wait for it!'

The two women, who had in fact bought an apron for her, pretended to be surprised and embarrassed.

'You didn't think of us then?'

Bachisia gave a shriek of laughter, but then grew serious again when Giovanna did not come out of her depression.

'No, we never thought about you. But Giovanna will let you see some of the things we bought.'

Giovanna got up, lit the candle, and went into the next room. Brontu followed her with burning eyes, and Martina thought she had gone to fetch the present. Several minutes passed and Giovanna did not return.

'What are you doing in there?' asked Brontu.

'Nothing.'

Another minute passed.

'I'm going to see,' he said, standing up.

'No, no,' said Bachisia faintly, but Martina turned to her and said, 'Ssh, ssh.'

Brontu tiptoed through the door. Giovanna stood in front of the open chest reading a letter that she had found pushed under the door. It was from Costantino. In rough simple language he begged Giovanna for the last time not to do what she was about to do. Reminding her of the long gone days of their love, he promised to return, swearing his innocence. 'If you don't pity me,' he ended, 'pity yourself, your own soul, think of the mortal sin, think of eternity.'

Porredda's very words, her very words. The letter must have been pushed under the door by Isidoro, for it was a long time since Giovanna had had direct news from the prisoner. Tears filled her eyes, more perhaps at the thought of the past than of eternity. Suddenly she heard the door open and someone enter softly. Quickly she bent down, pretending to rummage in the cupboard, her hands trembling and her eyes misty. Brontu came up behind her and grasped her by the shoulders, and she trembled all over.

'What are you doing?' he murmured in a hoarse voice.

'Oh, I was just looking for the apron for your mother. I don't know where I put it. Leave me alone. Leave me alone,' she said, trying to free herself from his eager arms. As she turned she saw Brontu's teeth gleaming between his smiling red lips, glossy as cherries, and she closed her eyes as if hiding from the temptation to kiss him. Then she felt his hand behind her head and his lips fierce as fire found her own.

'We aren't thinking of eternity,' she said fearfully, as soon as he had kissed her.

They went back into the kitchen, and soon she began to laugh with the fresh pure laugh of a young girl, while Brontu looked at her with the special expression he had when he was drunk.

Winter passed. Costantino's friends went on plotting, for the ill-starred marriage had not yet taken place. But the Dejas and the Eras seemed driven by fate. They were unyielding, and neither prayers, threats, nor gossip could move them.

The mayor, himself a shepherd, a pale proud man who looked a little like Napoleon, protested against the marriage and when he met Giovanna or Brontu he would spit on the earth in contempt. Before the love-affair had come to light people had always muttered, but now they were delighted to have a real piece of scandal to gossip about. When the question of marriage arose they laughed, thinking it would never happen and supposing that Brontu was making mock of the Era women. Even so, they might have said nothing more had Brontu and Giovanna simply lived together – it would have been neither the first nor the last case of this, and Giovanna would have been forgiven because she was young and poor – but to marry a woman who was already married! That the people could not tolerate. Some threatened to make a scene, to throw stones, to hiss and boo, to beat the couple on the wedding day. And they knew it. Brontu was enraged. Bachisia said 'Leave it to me,' and Martina lifted her head like a mare sniffing the dust of an explosion. She felt she was growing old, she was tired of working, and wanted an unpaid servant in the house. Giovanna suited her very well. Brontu must take her, no matter if people burst with envy.

No one knew where or by whom the marriage was to be celebrated. Some said it was to be in a country church, by a drunkard priest to whom Brontu had given a pair of oxen. There was a great deal of laughter at this detail, but at whose expense, the first or the second husband, no one really knew.

One night Isidoro Pane was at work in his tumbledown hovel by the bright light of a large, cheerful fire. He had gathered the wood himself from the fields, the river bank, and the woods. During the winter he plaited rope out of horsehair. He could do anything – sewing, spinning, cooking (when there was anything to cook), cobbling shoes. But he remained poor. Suddenly the door opened, revealing a slice of the clear but

95

sombre March night, and Giacobbe Dejas came in and sat silently beside the fire.

The fisherman's kitchen glowed as if it were burning, and the red light picked out the two figures and other objects in the room, leaving the rest in darkness. In one dark corner was a large, greyish cobweb, with a spider in the middle of it. In the corner of the hearth stood a glass jar, brimming with water, in which black leeches swam. A yellow basket was propped against the wall and the old fisherman sat with a rope of frayed black horsehair between his reddened, bony fingers.

'How are you now?' asked Giacobbe.

'How am I?' answered the old man. 'I don't know.'

'They've done it now,' went on Giacobbe as if talking to himself. 'It's done, finished. The drunkard didn't even come to the sheepfold today. I went home too. Well, why should I waste my time? I couldn't care less about the sheep. I came here. We must do something, Isidoro. Isidoro, leave that rope alone and listen to me. We must do something. Do you agree?'

'I agree. But what can we do? We've done everything we can. We've shouted, prayed, threatened. The mayor tried, the secretary, Father Elias.'

'That Father Elias. What's he done? He prayed, but he sweetened his prayers with sugar. He's the one who should have threatened them. He should have said, "I will bring the holy books and curse you, I will excommunicate you. Neither water, nor bread, nor any other thing will ever satisfy you. You will live a life of hell." Then you'd see the result. But no, Father Elias is a fool, a milksop priest. He didn't do his duty. Don't talk to me about him or I'll fly into a rage.'

Isidoro put down the rope. 'There's no point in working yourself up,' he said. 'Father Elias should not have threatened them and he didn't. Believe me, excommunication will fall on that house of its own accord.'

'I'm going to leave. I'm going away. I don't want any more of their cursed food,' said Giacobbe, wrinkling his face in disgust. 'But first I want to have the pleasure of beating that vile pair.'

'You're mad, my little chicken!' said Isidoro, with a sad smile.

'Yes, I'm mad. What do you care? You didn't lift a finger to

96

prevent this unholy thing from happening. What a disgusting event. My happiness is all gone.'

'And you've aged ten years.'

'I keep thinking that Costantino will tell us we should have stopped it. Is it true he's ill?'

'Not now. He was. But he is certainly suffering a lot,' said Isidoro, shaking his head. Then he took up the rope again and he murmured, 'Excommunication, excommunication.'

'I'm so angry it makes me froth at the mouth,' went on Giacobbe, raising his voice. 'I want to be there when the excommunication comes upon them, as it surely will. God punishes in life and death, this I know. I want to be there at the punishment. What are you working on?'

'A horsehair rope.'

'Oh, a horsehair rope. Who are you going to sell it to?'

'I'm going to take it to Nuoro and sell it to the peasants, who will use it to make halters for oxen. Why are you looking at it like that? Do you want to hang yourself?'

'No, my little chicken, you can hang yourself, if God wishes. So,' he went on raising his voice, 'it seems that they are already married.'

The two were silent again. Then Isidoro said, 'Who knows? I still hope the wedding won't take place. I trust in God and in San Costantino for a miracle.'

'A miracle, exactly,' said the other in an ironic voice.

'Why not? What if one of these days the real murderer of Basilio Ledda were dying and were to confess on his death-bed? The prison sentence would end.'

'Exactly. One of these days,' replied Giacobbe, still ironically. 'You're as innocent as a three-year-old child.'

'Who knows? Perhaps we'll find out.'

'Just so. One of these days. Who can find out? How?'

'Who? I, you, someone else.'

'You are as innocent, not as a child of three, but as a snail when it first comes out of its shell. How can we find out? What's more, are we quite sure it wasn't Costantino?'

'Oh, we're quite sure,' said Isidoro. 'Any one of us could have done it, except him. It could have been me, or . . . you – '

Giacobbe got up to leave. 'What can be done then? Is there any remedy? You tell me.'

'Anyone except him,' repeated Isidoro, without raising his head. 'There is a remedy. Put it into God's hands.'

'Oh, you drive me mad,' cried Giacobbe, prowling about the hovel. 'I ask you what we can do about it and you say that to me, like a fatuous fool. I'll go and strangle Bachisia Era, that'll do it.'

He left as he had come, without greeting or farewell, seriously angry. Isidoro did not even raise his head, but Giacobbe had left the door open and after a few minutes the fisherman got up to shut it and stood on the threshold.

The March night was warm, moonlit but cloudy. He could already smell the damp scent of burgeoning vegetation. Around his hovel the hedges and the wild plants seemed to slumber in the eerie light of the moon. On the horizon, among diffused milky vapours, meandered a wavy line of clear sky that looked like a blue river on a sandy plain with a few nocturnal fires along its banks. Isidoro closed the door and, sighing, returned to work.

XI

It was the Eve of the Assumption, a torrid, cloudy Wednesday. Martina was spinning under the portico and Giovanna, who was pregnant, was winnowing the corn. Although this job usually took two women, she had to do it by herself, stirring the grain in the sieve to remove the grit, and then winnowing carefully over a cloth placed inside a basket. Giovanna sat on the ground, the basket in front of her, and beside her another basket full of dusty golden grain.

Instead of filling out, the 'wife with two husbands', as she was now called in the village, had grown thinner. Her nose was red and swollen, dark patches ringed her eyes, and her lower lip pouted in disgust. A handful of bedraggled hens crowded round the basket, trying to thrust their beaks into it, sometimes fluttering into the air and leaving feathers on the ground. Giovanna shouted and cursed at them to go away, and they would run off and stand ready, one claw raised, to return to the fray as soon as the young woman ceased paying attention to them.

She was very distracted. Her eyes were sad or, rather, indifferent, as if her mind were obsessed with her own ills. Nothing else interested her. She was barefoot now and rather dirty, because Martina was stingy with the soap.

The two women did not speak, but Martina kept her eye on Giovanna, and when the girl did not manage to scare off the hens in time, it was the old woman who screamed at them.

One of the tiresome creatures climbed up on to the edge of the basket and pecked into it.

'Get away!' screamed Martina, Giovanna swung round, and

the hen flapped its wings and flew off carrying a little piece of grain. Afraid, as always, that her mother-in-law would shout at her, she stretched out an arm to grab the grain, moaning, 'Oh, they're so tiresome.'

'They are indeed tiresome,' said Martina gently. 'No, don't stretch like that, my dear, you'll hurt yourself. I'll go.'

She left her spindle and, grain by grain, picked up all the scattered corn, while a hen pecked the wool on the distaff.

'I hope all your feathers drop out!' screamed the old woman, rushing up to it, and the hen took advantage of the situation to help her pick up the grain.

Head bent, silent, absorbed, Giovanna sieved the corn. From the portico could be seen the deserted yard, Bachisia's little cottage, purple in the pale grey light of the cloudy afternoon, a strip of the empty village, the empty yellow fields, and the leaden horizon.

Cloud upon cloud hung in the sky, giving out a great heat and silence that was too intense. In front of the portico a tall, barefoot man passed by driving two little black oxen; then a young girl, also barefoot, who looked at Giovanna with her big clear eyes; then a fat white dog, its nose to the ground. Nothing else broke the silence, the heavy, threatening sultriness.

Giovanna sieved and winnowed the corn more and more slowly. She was tired, and she was hungry, but it was not food she craved. She was thirsty, but not for water. She felt an inexplicable physical need for she knew not what.

Finishing her work, she got up and shook her jacket, leaned down, and began to tip the grain from one basket into the other.

'Leave it, leave it,' said Martina solicitously. 'You'll hurt yourself.'

She would not even allow the girl to carry the corn to the grinding machine – a mill driven by a donkey, that milled a hundredweight of grain every four days. She insisted on doing it herself. Left alone, Giovanna went into the kitchen, looked around, rummaged here and there. Nothing, nothing, no fruit, no wine, not a drop of liquid to satisfy the inexplicable thirst that tormented her. There was only a little coffee and she heated it up, putting into it a spoonful of sugar from a sack. Then carefully she covered up the fire again.

The hot drink seemed to increase her thirst. She would have liked something cool and sweet that she had never tasted and would never taste. A dumb, deaf anger took hold of her. Her eyes gleamed. She went to the door of the storeroom and shook it, although she knew it was locked, and with pale lips she cursed under her breath.

Then she went out, barefoot as she was, crossed the yard silently and called to her mother.

'Come in,' said Bachisia from the kitchen.

'I can't. I can't leave the house empty.'

Bachisia came out, looked at the sky, and said, 'It's going to rain tonight. There's going to be a storm.'

'I wish all the thunder in the sky would come down,' said Giovanna savagely. 'Except what I carry in my heart.'

'You're in a bad mood, my dear. Where's the old witch gone? I saw you were winnowing the corn.'

'She's gone to take it to the grindstone. She's afraid to let me go in case I steal it.'

'Be patient, dear, it won't always be like this.'

'Yes it will. Always. What sort of life is this? She has honey on her lips and a goad in her hand. Work, work, work. She drives me like a draught beast. Barley bread and water and sweat and darkness in the evening and bare feet as much as I like.'

Bachisia listened helplessly. These complaints were an everyday affair. Bachisia too had to work harder than ever before, but she did not complain about it. It was only Giovanna's truly miserable state that grieved her.

'Be patient, be patient, my dear. We'll see better times. No one can take the future from you.'

'What does the future matter? I'll be old then – if I don't die of rage first. What's the use of being well-off when you're old? There's no happiness now.'

'I'd like to be happy too,' said her mother. 'And I'd like to have no work to do. I'd like to eat roast meat, soft bread, trout, eels, to drink wine and cordial and hot chocolate.'

'Stop it,' cried Giovanna with a spasm of anger. She told her mother how she could find nothing in the house to satisfy her unbearable thirst and hunger.

'Be patient. It's because of your condition. Even if you had the best food in the world, fit for a king, you wouldn't feel satisfied.'

Giovanna kept looking towards the portico with sad eyes and a sneer of disgust on her lips.

'It's going to rain tonight,' she said again.

'Let it rain then.'

'Will Brontu come back?'

'Yes, and tonight I'm going to tell him. Yes, I'm going to tell him.'

'What do you want to tell him, my dear?'

'I want to tell him I can't go on, that he took me to turn me into a servant, he's cheated me, and that, that – '

'You're not going to tell him anything!' exclaimed the old woman fiercely. 'Leave him alone. He works too, he too lives like a servant. Why do you want to torment him? He could throw you out, marry another woman. Wait until this blessed law arrives. Then you'll be the mistress.'

Giovanna shook uncontrollably. Then she calmed down, and tears came into her eyes. 'He's not a bad man,' she said. 'But he's always drunk, he's always swilling grappa, and he revolts me, and he flares up for no reason. He's disgusting, really disgusting. I ought to have . . . It would have been better – '

'What would have been better?'

'Nothing.'

It was always the same. Giovanna's thoughts returned again and again to Costantino, so good, so handsome, so courteous and kind, and once more she yearned for the past. A misery more bitter than death enveloped her soul, and the thought of the coming birth did not soften it – indeed, it increased her sorrow monstrously.

Evening fell, sombre and grey. The sky was like a granite vault. Not a breath of wind broke the sultry silence. Giovanna went and sat on the stone under the motionless almond tree, and her mother sat down beside her. They were silent awhile, then the young woman said, as if continuing a conversation, 'It happened during the first months of his sentence. It's the same now. Every night I dream of his return, and, oddly enough, I'm not afraid, although Giacobbe Dejas says that if Costantino returns he'll kill me or have Brontu and me put in prison. I don't know, my heart tells me that he will return. At first I didn't believe it, but now I do. Oh, it's useless to look at me like that. Do you think I'm accusing you? It's I who should be afraid of your accusations. Are you happy about me? You can't be. You never come to see me in that house' – and she stuck out her lip to indicate the white house – 'because my mother-in-law is afraid you'll take out some dust on your feet. I can't give you anything. Nothing. Do you understand – nothing at all, not even my work. Everything is closed to me. I'm the servant.'

'But I don't want anything, my dear. Why are you making yourself miserable for such a foolish reason? I don't need anything,' said Bachisia in a gentle voice. 'Don't worry about me. It's only the debt to Anna-Rosa Dejas that worries me. I'll never manage to pay her. But she'll be patient.'

Giovanna reddened with anger, wrung her hands, and raised her voice.

'That's what I wanted to say to that filthy animal tonight. At least pay for the rags I wear. Pay for them, and may a bullet pierce your heart.'

'Don't raise your voice, my dear. It's no good getting worked up. He might throw you out.'

'Let him throw me out. I hope he does. At least I could work for myself, and for you, not for those damned people. Oh, here she comes,' she said, lowering her voice, because the black shape of Martina had appeared on the pale background of the yard. 'Now she'll scold me because I left the house empty. She's afraid the money'll be stolen. She's got so much, she doesn't even know how much she's got. She can't tell the notes apart, nor the coins. She's got ten thousand *lire*, a thousand *scudi* – '

'Two thousand.'

'Well then, two thousand *scudi* hidden. And I don't even have a drink to cool me down, and I feel burned up inside.'

'It'll be all yours,' said Bachisia, 'be patient, wait. When the angels take her to paradise, it'll all be yours.'

Giovanna coughed, scratched her neck, and rested, breathing heavily.

'I wish they'd throw me out, I don't care. Now the secretary of the commune, that half-priest, says that I am Brontu's real wife, but I feel as if I were living in mortal sin with him. Remember how we got married? On the quiet, in the dark, without even a dog, without a feast, with nothing. Giacobbe Dejas – I hope he chokes – laughed and said, "Let the battle begin," and the battle has begun.'

'Listen,' Bachisia's voice was low and urgent, 'don't be foolish. You've always been crazy and you always will be. It's foolish to be so desperate. All poor daughters-in-law live like you do. There'll be a harvest time for you too. Be patient, be obedient, everything will pass. Wait until the baby is born. Then things will change.'

'Nothing will change. At least up until now I didn't have children. Soon that'll be another burden to drag about with me, to crush me. Do you want to hear what I say? My real husband is Costantino Ledda.'

'You don't know what you're talking about. Shut up, or I'll stop up your mouth.'

'Even if he returns I won't be able to go back to him, because I'll have someone else's children.'

'And I'll stop up your mouth,' repeated Bachisia, fuming. She got to her feet and lifted her hand as if to carry out her intention, but there was no need, because Giovanna saw her mother-in-law crossing the yard and she fell silent.

Martina was spinning as she walked and she came slowly up to the two women. 'Enjoying the fresh air?' she said, still watching her spindle turning.

'Lovely and fresh. We're dying of heat. But it'll rain tonight,' replied Bachisia.

'It'll certainly rain. I hope it doesn't thunder. I'm so afraid of thunder. It's the devil unloading sacks of walnuts. Let's hope Brontu will be back soon. What shall we make for dinner, Giovanna?'

'Whatever you like.'

'Do you want to stay here? Don't harm yourself. You might harm yourself.'

'What do you want me to do?'

'The evening air is always harmful. It's better to be inside now, and you can always make the dinner. There are eggs, my girl, eggs and tomatoes. Prepare them for yourself and your husband. I don't feel hungry,' she went on, turning to Bachisia. 'I hardly ever feel hungry. It must be the weather.'

'And it's the devil who's prodding you in the backbone, and meanness that stops you from eating,' thought the other woman.

Giovanna said nothing. She sat motionless, sunk in a heavy dream.

'It's the Assumption Day sermon at eleven o'clock tomorrow. It's an inconvenient time. Are you going, Giovanna? It used to be at ten o'clock.'

'I'm not going,' replied Giovanna in a dull voice. She was ashamed to go into the church nowadays.

'Yes, it's hot by then. It's better you don't go. If I'm not wrong, it's raining,' said Martina, holding out a hand. A large drop of dirty water fell and spread on the back of her pallid hand. More drops fell on to the almond tree and on to the ground, pitting the sandy yard. Then a yellow glow lit up the sky. Against a background of grey clouds a huge yellow cloud passed, laden with water like an enormous sponge.

The women went inside, and suddenly it began to pour down in torrents, straight and violent without wind or thunder. The shower only lasted ten minutes, but the whole village was flooded.

'Oh God and San Costantino, Oh Holy Assumption,' groaned Martina. 'If Brontu is on the way home he'll be wet as a day-old chick.' She looked anxiously at the sky, but did not stop spinning.

Giovanna began to prepare the dinner. Listening to the noise of the rain, she too felt afraid – not for her husband, but of a strange, unknown danger. The yellow glow that had accompanied the downpour mingled with a bluish light that came out of the west. The rain stopped at once, the clouds opened, separated, and sailed away, one behind the other, like people dispersing after a big meeting in the square. Through the freshened air came a grey gleam, a smell of earth and of newly bathed dry grass, and the cocks, thinking it was dawn, began to crow. Then silence fell. Martina was still spinning under the portico. Giovanna crouched on the hearth and was lighting the fire when she heard a whinnying coming through the air. Trembling, she got up and looked outside. Brontu had returned, and she was afraid.

In Bachisia's cottage a light shone, and the old woman could be seen pushing the water out of the doorway of her house with a furze broom. Beyond the fields the horizon looked like a strip of sea, green and calm. The dripping almond tree loomed over the whole scene and beneath its branches, in the last glow of the day, appeared Brontu on his horse. Horse and rider were black and steaming, lagging along as though sodden and weighted with water.

The two women, uttering half-hearted noises of sympathy, went out to meet him. The man ignored them. 'Hell and damnation,' he murmured. He pushed his feet out of the stirrups and jumped down from the saddle, absolutely soaked. 'Deal with this,' he ordered, striding into the kitchen. The two women unsaddled the horse, then Giovanna came in, and Brontu at once asked for a drink to dry himself out.

'Get changed,' she said.

He didn't want to change his clothes. All he wanted was a drink to dry himself. At first he grew angry when Giovanna insisted. Then, in the end, he did what she wanted. He changed, without having a drink, and while he waited for supper he dried his hair with a rag and combed it neatly.

'What a downpour, what a downpour,' he said. 'It's soaked me right through to the bone this time,' and he gave a little laugh. 'How are you feeling, Giovanna? Giacobbe Dejas sends you greetings. You're like smoke in the eyes to him.'

'You should curb his tongue,' said Martina. 'If you were any use you'd be respected by that trash of a shepherd.'

'I'll curb more than his tongue. He wanted to come back

tonight. Let him stay there and rot. He can come back tomorrow.'

'Tomorrow morning? He shouldn't even come tomorrow morning. You let yourself be robbed blind, my son, and you won't lift a finger. You're a good-for-nothing.'

'After all,' said Brontu, combing his hair, 'tomorrow is the Assumption, and Giacobbe is a member of the family. Be quiet now. Look, Giovanna, aren't I beautiful?'

He smiled at her, showing his teeth. He was indeed handsome and clean, with gleaming hair. Giovanna felt herself growing tender towards him. He began to hum a song that children sing when it rains:

'Rain, rain, the pouring rain,
The grape and the fig are ripening again.'

Then they ate happily and contentedly. Martina, claiming she had no appetite, ate quite greedily – bread, onions, and cheese. After supper Brontu asked Giovanna to go out for a walk with him, and they wandered, going nowhere in particular, through the narrow empty village streets. The sky had grown crystal clear, a shooting star draped a golden thread across the horizon, and the scent of the shrubs and the soaked stones quivered in the air. The alleyways were full of sand and mud, but Giovanna had wide, clumsy shoes that clattered on the stones. Brontu took her arm and tried, as he often did, to amuse her with wild tales.

'Do you know what Zanchine found? A baby.'

'When?'

'Today, I think. Zanchine was rooting out a mastic stump when he heard a crying noise. He searched around. It was a baby of a few days old. But now comes the good part: a small cloud sped through the air and, growing bigger and bigger, dropped down over Zanchine and grabbed the child. It was an eagle. It must have stolen the baby from somewhere and hidden it in the scrub. When the bird saw Zanchine pick up the child, it swooped.'

'Go on with you,' said Giovanna. 'I don't believe a word of it.'

'May I grow rich if it's not true.'

'Get away,' she repeated, irritated with him. Brontu realized

107

that she was upset rather than amused, and he asked her if she'd been having bad dreams. She remembered the dream she had had and did not reply. They came to Isidoro Pane's hovel. In the east the moon showed its big golden face against a silver sky, and the black earth, the sodden trees, the stone cottages, the heath and the whole wild plain, right up to the furthest line of the horizon, glistened like the smile that follows tears.

As the two young people passed the fisherman's cottage, they heard Isidoro singing a hymn. Brontu stopped.

'Let's go on,' said Giovanna, pulling him by the arm.

'Wait. I want to knock on that thing which passes for his door.'

'No,' she said urgently. 'Let's go, let's go. Come on or I'll leave you alone.'

'Oh, so it's true that you quarrelled with him. Not me though. I'm going to knock on his door.'

'I'm leaving then.'

'He's singing the hymn to San Costantino. The one the saint gave him on the river bank,' said Brontu, joining her. 'That old man is mad.'

She knew who had composed the hymn, and sadness came over her. Brontu took her arm again and began to joke and tell tall stories. He was in a good mood, but his laughter was lonely, for Giovanna would not utter a sound.

Anyone who had seen them go by and heard the jokes and Brontu's laughter might have thought that, despite everything, Giovanna was a very lucky woman. But she herself was absorbed in thoughts of Costantino.

XII

The church service began after ten o'clock the following day. It was late in starting because they had to wait for a young priest, a friend of Father Elias, to arrive from Nuoro. He was coming at his own expense to preach for the people of Orlei on this Feast Day.

By ten o'clock the little church was so crowded it was groaning at the seams. The interior was vibrant with colour. Brilliant turquoise bands streaked the pink walls. The yellow wood of the pulpit and the fair-haired, red-cheeked saints in their pink niches glowed brightly. Only the face of San Costantino, the patron saint, dressed as a soldier, was dark and severe. There was a legend in the village that this ancient statue, to which many miracles had been attributed, had been sculpted by San Nicodemo himself.

A shaft of light came through the open door, throwing a dusty halo over the heads of the crowd. The altar stood in semi-darkness, except for an 'M' picked out in burning candles, each flame like a golden arrow on a haft of white wood. Father Elias was celebrating the Mass. His friend, dressed in a lacy surplice, and with a face like a shrewd child, sang in a clear voice. The people were surprised to see the young priest who was to give the sermon singing. Many had come especially to hear him preach, although they listened with scant attention, whispering and casting curious looks around them. It was suffocatingly hot, and innumerable insects pestered the crowd. Having sung the Gospel, Father Elias turned his pale, calm face to the congregation and opened his mouth to speak.

At that moment, against the bright blue of the open

doorway, appeared the figure of Giacobbe Dejas, a sneer of triumph on his face. Observing that the priest was speaking, he stopped on the threshold of the door, his black cap in his hands. He could hear nothing. Walking forward, he said in a low voice to an old man, 'What's he been saying?'

'I didn't hear,' replied the old man testily. 'They're all babbling away as if it were the village square.'

A young man turned, looked at Giacobbe, and, observing his new suit and his malicious smile, said, 'I think Father Elias said the other priest is going to preach the sermon.'

'Did you hear him?' asked the old man petulantly.

'I didn't hear anything.'

Giacobbe passed between the rows of men, who followed him with their eyes. Silence descended on the crowd. The men leaned against the walls, while the women sat on the floor. In the centre of the church, in a beam of pearly light, was a sort of bed of blue wood, guarded at each corner by a rosy cherub with butterfly wings. Lying on brocade cushions on the bed was a small Madonna with closed eyes. Golden rings, earrings, and necklaces shone against her coat of blue satin. She was the Virgin of the Assumption.

The young priest climbed into the pulpit. Giacobbe Dejas stared at him, then he turned his head and cupped his right ear so as to hear better.

'People of Orlei, brothers and sisters,' said a childish but sonorous voice, 'I have been asked to preach a short sermon on this solemn day.'

Giacobbe enjoyed pretending to be deaf. He did not need to strain his ears; he could hear perfectly well. He turned to the congregation and, not missing a word of the sermon, began to address the assembly in his mind.

'Here we have that old devil Isidoro Pane, wearing a new suit too. Is he thinking of getting married? That young man with the red face at the back there laughed at me because I look happy dressed in my new clothes. They all say I'm going to be married. Well, what if I am? What business is it of yours, you gnawing dogs? Is there something wrong with that? I've got a house now and cattle. My sister will die without heirs, God bless her. She wants me to marry. All right, I'll get married, but who to? I'm hard to please. Also, I'm afraid. There's my young master – look at him with mortal sin on his face. What's he doing here? Why don't you beat him? Why don't you kick him out. And what about that old hawk, his mother. She's there too. Why don't you kick her out?'

'If they kicked out everyone who is in a state of mortal sin,' he thought, 'the church would be empty. But I hate those two. I'd beat them until I drew blood. But I'm not cruel. I arrived late today because I had to repair the dams that were broken in yesterday's downpour. When I came back I found Giovanna preparing the dinner. She was dirty and unhappy. It's no holiday for her. Mother and son went out. She, the servant, stays in the house and works. Stay there, die, you fallen woman. But I'm sorry for her. God forgive me, I'm sorry for her. I've said bad things to her. After all, she's the mistress and I'm the servant. Is it my fault, my little chicken, if I insult you? Let's listen to what that sparrow of a priest is saying.'

'Dear brothers and sisters,' said the priest in the soft northern accent with its touch of Spanish, waving his pale hands. 'Faith in Our Lady is the most sublime ideal. She, the gentlest lady, wife and mother of Our Lord, ascended to heaven, radiant and fragrant like a pink cloud, and sits now in glory among the angels and seraphim.'

'Look at Father Elias,' thought Giacobbe, turning back to face the altar, his slanted eyes glinting like steel. 'Look at him with his hands together in prayer. He knows no better than to preach goodness, when he has the holy books and could threaten to excommunicate Giovanna Era. He seems to have gone into a dream now.'

'No one has ever failed to receive grace when, in true faith, they have prayed to Our Most Holy Lady. She, the lily of the valley, the mystic Rose of Jericho,' went on the little priest, leaning out of the yellow pulpit.

'He'll never finish,' thought Giacobbe.

The people began to tire. Scattered here and there on the ground like buttercups and poppies, the women fidgeted and stopped listening. The young priest realized and finished his

111

sermon, blessing the shepherd people, who had heard God's word while their minds were on their own business, not to mention that of others.

Then Father Elias shook himself out of his daydream and took over the celebration of the Mass. Only he and Isidoro Pane had listened closely to the sermon. He ended the Mass and the fisherman began to sing the sacred hymns in his sonorous voice that was like clear water rushing between lone bushes of musk-rose.

The young priest listened ecstatically to the sonorous chanting. The old man with his long beard and gentle eyes, a bone rosary twisted on his gnarled fingers, reminded him of the figure of a pilgrim by the Dutch painter, Jan Both, that he had seen in Rome.

He asked to meet Isidoro, so Father Elias stopped the fisherman at the church door. Giacobbe watched, and seeing the old man's firm friendship with the priests, he felt an inexplicable jealousy. Waiting for Isidoro in the square, he said to him, 'I hope you get a bullet in your gaiters! What did they say to you?'

'They invited me to supper with them,' said Isidoro, not without a certain pride.

'Oh, so they wanted you to have supper with them? You've become a personage of some standing, my chicken. Look, come with me.'

'To the Dejas! Never,' said Isidoro angrily.

'No. Today I'm not going to eat the potato peelings thrown out by those scarecrows. I'm going to eat in my own house. Come on.'

He took Isidoro to his sister's house. It was after midday. The sun scorched the little alleyways where the mud had dried and the trees steamed in the fierce blue of the sky against the wild background. The people were going back home. The shepherds' heavy footsteps rang out on the cobbles, and children, dressed in their best, watched from the garden walls. Through open doors dark interiors of kitchens could be seen where copper saucepans shone like huge medallions. Spirals of smoke twisted into the clear air. All at once the sound of an accordion stole out from a normally deserted courtyard, as if played underground by some ancient, sombre fairy. The whole town had a holiday atmosphere, although there was a huge sadness about those wide, open doors, those spirals of smoke, the children awkward in their new clothes, the accordion music, the cottages unshaded in that hour of burning heat.

Giacobbe took the fisherman to his sister's house, where they all three ate together. A childless widow, the woman adored Giacobbe, still calling him 'little brother'. She knew nothing of evil and was terrified at the very thought of someone committing a sin. One of her greatest sorrows had been Giovanna's new marriage and, although she had lent the girl the money for her trousseau, it was perhaps against her better judgement. Her brother was always teasing her.

'Here's our friend Isidoro. He's thinking of taking a wife and has come to ask your advice,' he said to her.

'Bless you, Isidoro Pane, do you really want to get married?'

'Get on with you,' replied the fisherman good-humouredly.

'Then you don't want to get married?' called out Giacobbe, his strong teeth tearing a piece of roast pork that he held in his fingers. 'You filthy animal. He's got lots of sweethearts, sister.'

'I don't believe that.'

'May God strike me dead if I tell a lie. I swear he has lovers who suck his blood.'

Isidoro and the woman laughed, for of course Giacobbe was referring to the leeches.

Holding the meat between his teeth and his left hand, the shepherd hacked at it with his knife, complaining that it was as tough as the devil's ear. Having begun to laugh, the two others now found everything funny. Giacobbe, however, was not laughing. For some reason his earlier good humour seemed to have deserted him.

'Afterwards I'll take you to see my *palazzo*. It'll be ready in a few days, and if you would like to rent it you'll get lodgers soon enough. But I'm not going to rent it out, I'm going to live in it.'

'Are you going to give up your job?'

'Yes. I'm giving up my job. I've worked long enough. I've been working for forty years, you know. Forty years. No one can say I stole the money to live on in old age.'

'Are you going to get married?'

'Pooh, who'd want me? I'd spit in the face of any young woman who accepted me, and I don't want an old one. Drink, Isidoro Pane.'

'You'll make me drunk. Well, it's a holiday. I drink to the happy couple.'

'What happy couple?'

'Giacobbe Dejas and Bachisia Era,' said the fisherman gaily.

Giacobbe made as if to throw himself at Isidoro. 'I'll get you,' he cried, his little eyes green with fury.

'Help! Help! Murder!' cried Isidoro.

'Ssh! You mustn't say things like that,' said Anna-Rosa.

Giacobbe drank two glasses of wine, one after the other, and then laughed in a strained sort of way, his eyes on his sister and the fisherman.

'Why don't you two get married? My sister is rich. Look how fresh she is. She's like a rosebud. They say she found a miraculous herb and makes potions that keep her skin fresh.'

'You're in such a strange mood,' said his sister.

'Yes. Get married. I want you to. You shall have everything of mine because I'll die before my sister. I don't know why, but I think I'm going to die soon. I think I'm going to be killed.'

'Go on with you. It's the wine that's killing you today.'

'Little brother, whatever are you talking about? By the souls in Purgatory, whatever are you talking about?' exclaimed his sister in a terrified voice.

'You've no enemies,' remarked the fisherman. 'Only those who have lived by the sword die by the sword.'

'I have injured several creatures,' replied Giacobbe in a serious voice, sinking his teeth into a slice of melon. 'I see you don't understand. Sheep and lambs!' Then he raised his face, stained pink with melon juice, and laughed.

The two men went out to look at the new house. It had two floors, four large rooms, a kitchen, and a stable. It was quite big enough, however, for everyone in the village, including Giacobbe, to call it a *palazzo*.

114

'Look here, look here,' said Giacobbe, pointing out every nook and cranny, and his smooth, eyebrowless face became jovial again.

'Take my sister as your wife,' he repeated. 'This house will be yours.'

'You're teasing me because I'm poor,' replied the fisherman.

He trod cautiously across the wooden floor while Giacobbe stamped the iron heels of his boots, enjoying the echo that he raised in the big empty rooms that smelled of fresh whitewash.

The windows, whose stone sills burned in the sun, looked out over the whole village, blackish-brown, like a pile of spent charcoal, under its green veil of trees. Beyond lay the yellow plain and the great purple-grey sphinxes. In the burning afternoon silence, the incessant peal of the church bell sounded like the clang of a chisel working wearily away far-off in the centre of those mountains.

'Why don't you want to marry my sister?' asked Giacobbe, leaning out awkwardly over one of the window-sills. 'This house could be yours, this could be the bedroom. Here at this window, you could stand, smoking your pipe.'

'I don't smoke. Leave me in peace,' said Isidoro impatiently, for the shepherd's words were beginning to upset him. He too leaned out of the window.

'I'm not joking, you old lizard,' broke out Giacobbe. 'But you are so beggarly that it doesn't occur to you that I'm not joking.'

'Look here,' said Isidoro. 'Today you gave me dinner, and just because of that you want to joke at my expense. If you want me to go on being grateful, leave me alone.'

Giacobbe watched him for a while and then laughed.

'Let's go and have a drink now,' he said.

They went off, Giacobbe to the tavern and Isidoro to the church.

In the tavern Giacobbe found Brontu playing *morra* noisily with the other men. Long before five o'clock, when the procession was due to start, they were all drunk. Giacobbe was drunker than any of them, and he, thinking that Brontu was about to collapse at any moment, took the young master by the arm. He invited everyone in the tavern to come to his *palazzo* to watch the procession.

The huge empty rooms resounded with raucous voices, uncontrolled laughter, and staggering footsteps. The open windows filled with wild, flushed, bearded faces.

Giacobbe and Brontu leaned out of the window where the fisherman had stood. The sun had sunk down, but the window-sill was still hot, while away in the distance the mountains seemed more and more furrowed with purple shadows.

'Cooee!' shouted Brontu, his eyes rolling glassily. The others copied him, each man shouting louder than his neighbour. The street filled up with people curious to see what was going on, and soon a battle broke out with pebbles, spittle and swear words flying between the drunks at the windows and the drunks in the street. Suddenly silence fell. A grave chant rose up and then two rows of ghostly white figures appeared at the far end of the street, and a silver cross shone against the blue sky.

The men in the street drew back against the walls, the faces in the window gazed down and each man took off his cap. As the procession passed by, one of the white-clad boys – who later on would be given three *soldi* and a slice of melon – banged on the door of the new house, and all the others copied him as they followed.

'Damned louts,' said Giacobbe, leaning out of the window. 'Louts. Look at them, walking in the religious procession!' He was going to spit on them, but Brontu stopped him.

After the boys in white came a pale green embroidered banner with its mass of different coloured tassels, and then the gold staff. Next came the bed, on which lay the Madonna of the Assumption guarded by the little green angels. At each of the four corners of the bed, as well as the bearer, walked a man in a white tunic carrying a child dressed as a cherub. Two of the children were fair and two dark, and they chattered to each other loudly so as to hear above the noise. One, tickled under the knee by the man who was carrying him, laughed and wriggled, one of his wings dangling crookedly.

Giacobbe, Brontu and their companions knelt and crossed

themselves, looking tenderly at the four children. One of them recognized an uncle of his at the window and threw him a pink sugared almond that dropped back into the street.

Father Elias and the young priest from Nuoro, clothed in brocade and lace, looking pale and handsome in their elaborate robes, sang the Latin prayers.

'May the devil make a hole in your wallet, here's that filth of an Isidoro Pane,' said Giacobbe fidgeting. 'He looks as if he owns the procession. I'm going to spit on him.'

'Stop it,' ordered Brontu.

Giacobbe cleared his throat to catch the fisherman's attention but Isidoro did not even raise his eyes. As he walked he intoned the prayers, and the crowd responded, seeming to follow him like a flock of sheep their shepherd.

Bareheaded men, bald heads glistening with sweat, heads of thick, straight hair, heads of curly black hair, women's heads covered with flowered wool kerchiefs, or yellow, red and green spotted scarves, moved past. A lame old man, a woman with two children, three old women, a boy with a yellow flower in his mouth, moved slowly by to the sound of chanting. A cat with a small white face and big blue eyes stretched out its claws, then jumped on to the wall opposite Giacobbe's house.

'Too late,' Brontu said, waving to it. They all laughed noisily. Giacobbe asked them to leave and, as they would not go, pretended to chase them away with a stick dipped in whitewash. The tough, haughty men ran hither and thither through the rooms, up and down the stairs, jostling against each other, pushing, screaming, and laughing like children. They ran out into the street, and Giacobbe locked the door of the *palazzo* behind them. Then, in a crowd, they returned to the tavern. Brontu and the shepherd went home at dusk, taking turns to prop each other up.

Martina stood alone in the portico, her hands under her apron, reciting her rosary. When she saw the two men she neither moved nor spoke but shook her head gently, pushing out her lip as if to say, 'You're a fine sight.'

'Where's Giovanna?' cried Brontu.

'With her mother.'

'With her mother? That old witch. She's always there, dammit.'

'Don't shout, my son.'

'Can't I shout in my own house?' he bawled. Turning towards the yard he yelled, 'Giovanna! Giovanna!'

Giovanna appeared at once at the door of the cottage and came across the yard looking terrified. But as she came nearer the expression on her face changed to one of scorn and disgust. When she reached the two men she glared at them in hatred. Giacobbe laughed to himself, and Brontu's ears went red with anger.

'What's the matter? Have you got a pain?' said Giovanna.

'I expect he will have soon!' exclaimed Giacobbe.

Brontu's lips moved but he could not speak, and the anger passed as it had come, without reason.

'I want you with me,' he babbled. 'We weren't seen together at all today. What were you doing with your mother? Who was there?'

'No one, for goodness sake. Who do you imagine would come to our house?' she replied bitingly.

'So you've left the sheepfold all alone,' broke in Martina. 'Is that how you look after the master's business? You filthy scoundrel. There are thieves about.' Giacobbe got to his feet, pale and stiff, and would have hurled himself at the old woman, but Giovanna, afraid of what he might do, pushed herself between them.

Giacobbe sat down again without opening his mouth, but he had so terrified Giovanna that she stayed beside her mother-in-law in a defensive attitude. Then it was Brontu's turn to rant at his mother.

'What sort of manners are these? You treat people as if they were animals. Today was a holiday. Supposing we did get drunk? What does it matter to you?'

'I'm drunk with poison,' said Giacobbe.

'Yes, with poison. Me too,' said Brontu. 'I've had enough of mothers, wives, everyone. I'm going. I'm going to stay in Giacobbe's *palazzo*. After all, we're cousins.'

'That's what you think,' shouted Giacobbe. 'You're relying

on my heredity.' He started to howl with fiendish, sinister laughter. Brontu too began to laugh, trying to copy the shepherd's howl, but his guffaws were more like the joyful yelps of an animal in the month of May.

Giovanna grew more and more frightened of the gathering darkness, of the loneliness weighing on the yard, of the two men turned by the wine into violent, disgusting beasts. She saw excommunication descending on them all, the shepherd who turned against his master, the son who insulted his mother, and on her, Giovanna, who hated them all.

Martina got up, went into the kitchen, and lit the lamp. Giovanna followed her and prepared the supper. They all ate together, and for a little while a calm fell over them. Brontu told the women how he had watched the procession from the window of Giacobbe's *palazzo* and made Martina smile at his foolishness. Then he wanted to caress his wife. But Giovanna's heart was full of bile. For her the holiday had been gloomier even than an ordinary day. She had worked, she had not been to church, nor had she even changed her clothes. As soon as she had allowed herself to go to her mother's house, they had called her back like a dog to the kennel.

Therefore she shook off Brontu's caresses and told him he was drunk. Giacobbe began to laugh again and his ill-mannered laughter annoyed Giovanna more and offended Brontu further.

'Why are you laughing, you filthy dog?'

'I could reply that your filth is worse, much worse, than mine. But all I'm going to say is that I'm laughing because I want to.'

'Then I'll laugh too.'

'Half-wits,' said Giovanna scornfully. 'You make me sick.'

Unable to bear her coldness any longer, Brontu exploded. 'What's the matter? You're getting on my nerves, you know. I caress you and you insult me. You should kiss the ground I tread on. Do you understand?'

Giovanna went pale.

'Why?' she hissed. 'Isn't it enough that I wait on you? I'm the servant here.'

119

'Yes, the servant. Go on being the servant then. What more do you want, woman?'

Giacobbe's slanted eyes gleamed. Giovanna got to her feet, her face pale and tragic, and she emptied out all the poison she had in her soul. She insulted her husband and her mother-in-law. She called them torturers, threatened to leave, to kill herself, cursed the hour she had come into that house, and in her fury she told of the debt to Giacobbe's sister.

The shepherd began to chuckle to himself and to reproach his sister half-playfully. Suddenly he stopped with a heavy face, and the black figure of Bachisia appeared in the doorway. Bachisia had heard her daughter screaming in the stillness of the night and she had come.

'Your daughter seems to have gone mad as far as I can see,' remarked Martina calmly.

Brontu withdrew into himself, beckoning to his mother-in-law to come in and calm Giovanna down. Bachisia started forward, but Giacobbe jumped to his feet, his face contorted by a mask of hatred. 'Get out of here!' he yelled, pointing his finger towards the door.

'Are you the master?' asked Bachisia.

'Out of here,' he repeated, and because Bachisia came on forward, he rushed at her.

She turned and ran. The shepherd followed her out and sat in Martina's place under the portico, wanting to burst out laughing again. But instead of a laugh there came from him a convulsive tearless sobbing.

XIII

That winter Giovanna gave birth to a frail, sickly baby, and Dr Porru came from Nuoro to stand as godfather at the baptism.

He arrived in a carriage, smiling, wrapped up like a bundle, and the villagers ran out to see him. He smiled at Brontu's friends and greeted them cheerfully, saying he had seen them in Nuoro, which pleased them a lot. One, however, remarked that he had never been there.

'Never mind,' replied the fat little lawyer. 'We'll see you there too one day.'

It was an ugly omen, because the men mostly went to Nuoro to attend the court of justice. All the same, Brontu's friend was pleased. Bachisia told Dr Porru that he had got fatter. 'So what!' he exclaimed, and they all laughed wildly.

The baptism took place with great pomp. For once in her life Martina had loosed her purse strings, and ordered wines and sweetmeats from Nuoro. She could not sleep at night as a result and she spent all day in fear and trembling in case someone stole her goods.

On the day of the baptism Giovanna got up and helped her mother-in-law to make the macaroni for the feast. Then she went back to bed and sat there leaning against the pillows, with the covers drawn up to her waist and wearing her bridal blouse and bodice. She also wore a brocade cap and her marriage shawls, and she looked drawn but beautiful, her eyes larger than usual.

To lay the table Martina had taken from a chest linen cloths that had not seen the light of day since they had been bought.

The baptism was arranged for eleven o'clock, and the

morning was freezing and foggy. Thick white mist hung from the sky, enveloping the village, whose streets were deserted and strewn with frozen puddles. An indescribable silence reigned over the open space in front of the Dejas house, where the almond tree's naked branches were sketched black against the fog.

Suddenly the yard came to life, invaded by a swarm of urchins bundled up in skins and rags, with red fringed caps, and overlarge shoes. Then came groups of shivering women, coughing and sneezing and smelling of smoke and soot.

The baptismal procession emerged from Martina's house, led by two children who, with an air of grave importance, bore two large wax candles adorned with red ribbons. Then came a woman carrying the new-born baby wrapped in a shawl and a cloth of green brocade like San Costantino's banner. The godfather followed in his cloak and a black and white shawl from which his pink face emerged smiling beatifically. The godmother, so tall that she looked like a shadow at sunset, had to bend down to speak to him. Beside her walked Brontu, shaven and happy, followed by the relatives and friends who tramped by making a noise like a troop of horses. Finally, freezing cold, with a tray under her arm, her hands in the slit of her skirt, and now and again sticking out her tongue to lick a drop of water that fell from her purple nose, came the godmother's little maid.

The urchins flanked the procession, watching the godfather eagerly. He smiled and joked with them, saying, 'Come along, Come along. What are you waiting for, you little winter grubs?'

'He's a cripple,' said one boy.

'Shut up,' said another.

The procession passed. The boys' faces lengthened. Some grew angry, others stood crying.

'Hey!' shouted one, but before he could go on the godfather threw a fistful of copper coins into the air. All the urchins threw themselves on to the money, shouting. Some fell, trampling the little maid, who began to curse and kick and punch. The copper rain, and the consequent assault of urchins, which grew ever more numerous, continued until the procession arrived at the little church, where Father Elias waited, chatting to the sacristan, who wore a red cassock. The sacristan was afraid that Father Elias, with his well-known leniency, would go back to the baby's home after the ceremony, and he urged him to be severe with Brontu Dejas and his whole family.

'Sir,' he said, 'you won't go back to the baby's home, will you? It's almost a bastard. It should not receive honours.'

'Go and see if they're coming,' said the priest.

'They're not in sight. You're not going to go, Your Reverence?'

'Are you going?' asked the priest with a smile.

'That's another matter entirely. I go for the food, not to honour that rabble.'

Shortly after, the procession arrived and the ceremony began. As soon as her bald, red little head was uncovered, the baby let out a bleating cry. Still smiling and holding the lighted candle, the godfather tried to remember the creed, because Giovanna had begged him to recite it carefully so that the baptism would be valid.

The urchins too had managed to get inside the church and had set up a rustle like a flock of moths. The godmother's maid with her tray and the woman who had carried the baby sat on the altar steps, anxiously waiting for the godfather's gift.

When the ceremony was over, the gifts given, the baby dressed again, there was a moment of uneasy waiting on the part of Brontu and his friends. Father Elias had gone into the sacristy to disrobe. Would he come out? Would he come back to the house with them?

He did not come out again and the procession left rather gloomily, followed by the triumphant sacristan, to whom Brontu felt like giving a dose of bitter lime instead of sweetmeats. The people came out to watch the procession, and many, especially the women, smiled spitefully when the priest did not appear. It was like the baptism of a bastard. Although she had not really expected the priest to come, Giovanna went pale when the procession entered the room and she kissed the baby sadly.

'I remembered the creed right to the very last word,' said Dr

123

Porru. 'Cheer up, cousin. Your baby will be a portent – tall as her godmother, happy as her godfather.'

'Perhaps as lucky as her godfather,' murmured Giovanna.

'Now for supper,' exclaimed the young lawyer, rubbing his hands. 'A fine custom this, upon my word, very fine.'

He clapped his hands again as if summoning children, and they all sat down to the table before the macaroni, which was followed by a whole roast piglet that gave out an aroma of rosemary.

A few days later a strange incident took place. Beside Isidoro Pane's house was an ancient muck heap almost solidified by time. Strange pale grass and the sickly white stalks of rank weeds covered it. It had grown into a sort of knoll, and it no longer gave off any smell at all.

One evening at dusk, Isidoro Pane was preparing his supper when he heard a noise coming from the direction of the knoll, and he hurried to the door to look out into the cool greenish twilight.

A group of people, mostly women, black against the clear sky, was walking towards the muck heap, playing and singing. Isidoro realized what was going on, and he went out to meet them. There were about twenty women, old and young, and they were singing a harsh, melancholy chant, or spell, against the tarantula's bite, accompanying themselves on a primitive lyre, whose sounding-box was made from the dried bladder of a pig. The musician was a young blind beggar, dressed in the ragged dirty clothes of a woman.

Three men emerged from the group, one of them flushed and feverish, with a bandaged hand. Isidoro recognized him as Giacobbe Dejas. The fisherman touched the bandaged hand with a finger, while Giacobbe looked at him with terror-stricken eyes.

'I'm frightened I'm going to die. I've been bitten by a tarantula,' he said.

The women, seven widows, seven married women, and seven girls, went on singing. Among the widows was Giacobbe's sister, still pink and fresh-faced in spite of the heavy sorrow that had fallen on her. Her fine, strong voice rang out above all the others, strident as a cricket's.

'Saint Peter he went down to the sea
And behind him dropped his key.
Said God, "What is it, Peter mine?"
"She has bitten my foot, my heart, my spine."
"Take the sad thorn* and grind and pound,
And in three days you'll be safe and sound."
Tarantula with the spotted breast,
Your mean daughter you laid in the nest.
High on the hill you left one child,
Another you left in the valley wild.
One in the dale, one on the hill,
For you and I each other to kill.'

Still singing, the group approached the pile of old dung. The two men, who were armed with mattocks, began to dig a hole, while Isidoro stayed with Giacobbe amongst the singing women and the blind man who played the lyre.

Giacobbe watched the two men in silence while Isidoro, for his part, stared at the sick man, who seemed like another person, so changed was he. His face was red and inflamed, lined with anxious suffering. His usually shrewd little eyes, under their bare brows, were clouded with a childish fear of death. When they reached the last line the women began again from the beginning, and the music of the strange lyre took up the strident, monotonous theme, like the buzzing of many bees. The cold wind had frozen the sweat on him. His face had grown pale and his teeth chattered. They made their way to Anna-Rosa's house, and Isidoro, who had completely forgotten his dinner, followed the oddly-assorted group.

'Did you kill it?' he asked the sick man, remembering that anyone who kills a tarantula with his ring finger has the power of healing a bite with a touch of that finger.

Ispina triste or *santa*, from which Our Lord's crown of thorns is said to have been made. In Sardinia the leaves of this plant are used for medicinal purposes. [Tr.]

'No,' said Giacobbe. Then, as the lyre played on and the women sang, he told Isidoro in a few precise words how this accident had happened. 'I was asleep, I felt a prick like the sting of a wasp. I awoke sweating to find I'd been stung by a horrible tarantula. I saw it with these very eyes, but it had climbed the wall and was already high up. I hope the devil bites it, the bitch. I came back to the village, but now I'm frightened I'm going to die. For a long time I've been afraid of dying.'

'We are all going to die when the hour comes,' said Isidoro gravely.

'Yes, we're all going to die,' agreed one of the friends, but this was no comfort to Giacobbe Dejas.

'My legs feel shattered,' he said dolefully. 'And my backbone! It feels as if someone had stuck a hatchet in my backbone. I'm dying! I'm dying!'

The village people came out into the street to watch the group, and they stood there silently, as if watching a funeral pass by. Giacobbe's eyes clouded over and he stumbled and leaned heavily against Isidoro.

The women trotted on like fillies, and the melancholy song floated out in the cold evening silence broken by the strident tone of the lyre.

At last they reached the little widow's house where, on a stone hearth, in the centre of the kitchen, a fire burned. A number of pairs of breeches hung drying in front of the oven, which was a huge, vaulted affair with a hole at the top to let the smoke out. The oven filled up one whole corner of the room, and it had a square doorway, easily big enough for a man to crawl in. Giacobbe ducked down and climbed inside the warm oven, and through the opening the metal soles of his shoes could be seen, their hobnails shining in the fire's reflection.

Still chanting, the women gathered round the hearth, the firelight flickering and glinting on their yellow bodices and white blouses. Anna-Rosa's round, open mouth itself looked like a little black oven in her shining pink face. The blind man had felt the heat of the fire and he went up to it slowly still playing, and, reaching the hearth, he put his bare foot on the hot stone.

126

Isidoro whistled. 'Look out you don't burn yourself, boy.'

Hardly were the words out of his mouth when the lyre-player leapt backwards shaking his scorched foot. For a moment he stopped playing. The women danced on, their tall figures swaying around the fireplace, and it was as if they were intoning a funeral dirge around a prehistoric tomb.

'Come out now,' said Anna-Rosa, after a while.

Giacobbe's large feet emerged from the oven and at that moment the door of the house opened and a black figure appeared. It was Father Elias. Someone had come to warn him of what was going on, and he had run to the widow's house to prevent Giacobbe from being put into the oven. He was red and trembling, his eyes flashing.

One woman screamed. Most of the others went silent, but some tried to go on singing. At last Giacobbe came out of the oven.

'Quiet!' ordered the priest in a trembling voice. 'Have you no shame?'

They grew silent. 'Go,' he went on, throwing open the door, and, holding it with one hand, he pushed the women out of the house. When they had left, he realized Isidoro was there, and sadness came into the priest's eyes.

'You too,' he said reprovingly. 'How could you? Don't you see how you have hurt this poor man? How could you?' he repeated as if to himself. Then he pulled himself together. 'Quickly, go and call the doctor. And you. To bed. At once.'

Giacobbe could have asked for nothing better. He had a high fever, he was shaking, and he could scarcely see. Isidoro went to fetch the doctor. He felt humiliated for, notwithstanding his good sense, his wisdom, and his religion, he could not understand what harm there was in trying to cure the bite of a tarantula by singing and playing the ancient rites used by the fathers and forefathers of the village since the days when giants lived in the *nuraghi.**

Nuraghi: massive, prehistoric, stone towers with narrow entrances sometimes interconnected by low tunnels. Unique to Sardinia, they still exist in considerable numbers. [Tr.]

In the street the women dispersed into groups of two or three and, gathering in the shadows, muttered together about the event. They were seriously upset about the priest's action, and one girl clapped her hands and sang,

'A thunderbolt has struck me
Oh, mother of the spider.'

It was the refrain that would have been chanted round the sick man's bed had Father Elias not arrived. One or two of them wanted to persuade Isidoro to let them continue, but he had gone striding off elsewhere, deep in thought.

XIV

The room where Giacobbe Dejas lay was unusually high and
so huge that the oil lamp did little to light up the corners. The
furniture, which was similarly massive, included a red wooden
cupboard that was as tall as the ceiling and loomed over the
room with a grave, thoughtful air. There was a high, wooden,
majestic-looking bed, with a yellowish cover that hung down
to the floor. It was a mysterious room with its dark corners and
high, light-coloured ceiling like a cloudy sky. Anna-Rosa's
tiny figure seemed lost in the vast expanse, and she was
scarcely tall enough to see over the edge of the bed.

On that immense bed slept Giacobbe Dejas. In his fever he
thought that he was still in the hole in the ground and that the
two men who had buried him were piling earth around his
head, suffocating him. He was in agony, but he let them go on,
hoping he would be cured more quicky if he were completely
buried. His head was Father Elias, on whose chest moved the
tiny tail of a tarantula. In his dream the fear of death clutched
frenziedly at him. Lying in the warm oven he had thought that
hell might be a lighted oven, inside which the damned would
be stretched out for ever.

Now in his dreams the same feeling came over him. He was
buried in the hole, the earth piling up round his face, his
mouth shut tight so as not to swallow any, and then he saw the
lighted oven. It was hell. So great was his terror that, even in
his sleep, even in his fevered nightmare, something willed him
to realize that what he felt was just an illusion. And he woke
up, but with the same sensation that stones, had they any
feelings, would have in a fire. He felt as if he were burning, but

he could not move, could not flee his horrendous fate. He tried to scream, and his voice emerged from his mouth in a dull, low moan, but the sound of his own, human voice in the horrors of hell comforted him.

From the nearby kitchen where he lay sleeping Isidoro, who had stayed to help the widow in whatever way he could, heard that moan and was afraid. He awoke thinking that Giacobbe had died, and he got up and went into the sick man's room. Giacobbe lay still, his face strangely lengthened and his eyes glistening black with tears.

'Are you awake?' Isidoro asked softly. 'Do you want something?'

He touched the sick man's pulse, bending his head down as if to listen to the heartbeat. Suddenly, on the other side of the bed, Anna-Rosa's little face appeared, bound in a white kerchief. The sick man's face seemed to shrink, his mouth widened and his eyes squeezed shut. A long groan wheezed out into the room. The woman remembered how long ago as a child Giacobbe had sobbed on the selfsame bed. She reached out her hand and stroked the sick man's head, saying to him in a half-gentle, half-angry voice, 'The holy souls in Purgatory bless you, what's the matter? How do you feel, little brother?'

Isidoro went on trying to test the sick man's pulse, finding now one vein, now another. 'This is strange,' he said.

'What is it? Will you tell me what's the matter? What's the matter with you, Isidoro Pane?'

'Nothing, nothing. He called, that's all. Perhaps he had a bad dream. Let's give him some water. Bring some water. Drink, now. Look at him drinking. Are you thirsty? It's the fever, do you understand?'

When he had drunk the water, Giacobbe calmed down a little. An old gown of white cotton outlined his small wiry body. The thick black hair on his chest made a strange contrast with his bald head and hairless face. Frowning thoughtfully, he passed his good hand over his injured one and said in the fretful voice of the fevered, 'Horrible dream! Yes, yes, that's what it was. Dear San Costantino, how hot it is. The heat of the gallows. I dreamed of hell.'

'What an idea! What an idea!' said his sister reprovingly.

'Was it hot, little chicken?'

The sick man grew petulant. 'Don't tease me, don't say "little chicken" any more. It annoys me. I won't say it again. I'll never tease anyone again. Listen,' he went on, feeling his arm with his good hand. 'Hell is terrible. I'm going to die, and there's something I must tell you. Don't get worked up, Anna-Rosa – it's necessary for me to die. You know about it already, Isidoro, so I can tell you. It was I who killed Basile Ledda.'

Anna-Rosa's eyes and mouth widened in horror, and she leaned against the bed shaking convulsively.

'I knew nothing about it!' cried Isidoro.

Giacobbe lifted his head and began to tremble too. 'Don't have me arrested,' he pleaded. 'I'm going to die anyway. Do you really mean what you say? I thought you knew. What's the matter, Anna-Ro? Don't be afraid, don't have me arrested.'

'It's not that,' she said, pulling herself together somewhat. She felt as if she had been hit on the head. Her soul seemed to have left her and been replaced by another soul that saw the world, life, and God in a different way, and everything the new soul saw was full of horror, darkness and chaos.

'Of course I won't say anything. But I knew nothing about it. How could I have known?' protested Isidoro. He felt no horror of Giacobbe, indeed he felt pity for him. But at the same time he wished him to die. All at once each of them remembered Costantino, and from that time on the thought of him never left them for an instant.

'Lie down,' said Isidoro, patting the sick man's cheek with his hand. But Giacobbe shook his head and gabbled on in his fretful voice, sometimes begging, sometimes peevish.

'I thought you knew,' he said. 'So you didn't know? How could you have known? I was afraid of you, I thought you read it in my eyes. One night, in your house, you said to me, "It could have been you who killed Basile Ledda." I was frightened that evening. Then another day, Assumption Day, here in this house you called me a murderer. It was only a joke, but I was afraid of you. When I suggested you married my sister I was serious about it. I wanted to tie you to me.'

'Jesus Christ. Oh, Jesus Christ,' moaned the widow.

'You're afraid, eh?' said Giacobbe. 'Why did I do it, you ask? Well, because I hated that man. He beat me. He owed me money. But when they convicted Costantino I thought I would die. Why didn't I confess then? That's what you're saying. It's easier said than done. Costantino is a good lad. I will die before him. I'll confess all. What Giovanna Era did put a hundred years on me. What will Costantino say when he comes back? What'll he say?' he repeated in a subdued voice as if interrogating himself. 'What shall we do now?'

Anna-Rosa sighed. She felt as if she were caught in a terrible dream, but not for one instant did she think of hiding what her brother had revealed. Two equally dreadful possibilities awaited her. Either Giacobbe would die or he would be convicted. She did not know which would hurt her more grievously.

'Let's go to sleep now. Tomorrow we'll decide what to do,' said Isidoro. Again he patted the sick man's cheek. Giacobbe lay down and, raising his good hand, began to count on his fingers. 'Father Elias one. Then the mayor, then whats-his-name – Brontu Dejas. Yes, yes. Him too. I want them here. I'll confess to them.'

'To Brontu Dejas?' asked Isidoro, baffled.

'Because they'll believe him more than anyone. But first everyone must swear on the cross to let me die in peace. Will you do that for me?'

'Of course. Calm down. And you, cousin, go back to bed. Lie down, go to sleep,' said the fisherman in a gentle voice, adjusting the blankets round the sick man.

But Giacobbe shook his head restlessly. 'I'm hot, I'm hot. Let me be. Why are you not surprised, Sidore? I went on working as a shepherd so as not to cause suspicion. But you knew. Yes, yes, you knew.'

'I knew nothing, I tell you.'

'Why aren't you surprised then?'

'Many things happen in this world, but they are only earthly things. Now, stay covered up and try to sleep.'

The widow, who had not heard what the two men were

saying, raised her head. Her little face had grown lined and yellow. The years that had gone by peacefully without being able to furrow her forehead had taken their revenge in one second.

'Giacobbe,' she said, 'we don't need witnesses. We don't need to call anyone. Won't I be enough?'

He raised himself again and looked at Isidoro. Isidoro looked at him and said, 'She's right.'

A great calm seemed to spread through the strange yellowish room. The sick man lay back quietly and began to doze. The widow took Isidoro's advice and she too went to lie down. The tall cupboard once more loomed gravely out of the darkness, and the ceiling with its clouds pressed on the silence of the room as if on a deserted field. In their impassive calm all the objects in the room seemed to echo Isidoro's words – 'Only earthly things.'

The municipal doctor of Orlei, Dr Puddu, was a huge, puffy, bestial-looking man. Once, he too had nursed great ideals, but fate had set him down in this lonely village, where the people were seldom ill, and he had taken to drink, first just to keep himself warm, later because he developed a taste for wines and spirits. Now he was a complete alcoholic, and the inhabitants of Orlei had no more respect for him.

Giacobbe now complained of a pain in his side, and as Dr Puddu cauterized the hand bitten by the tarantula he talked to the sick man in a rough, grating voice.

'Fool. People don't die of such things. But if you die it'll be the way an ass dies.'

Grumbling angrily, Anna-Rosa watched the doctor. She had become ill-tempered, and anything connected with the invalid angered her. She seemed to have grown old since the previous night. Her once pretty little face was now more and more lined and yellow. Her brother's revelation had altered her physically and morally. Day and night she wondered in numb amazement how Giacobbe could ever have killed a man.

'He's as gay and gentle as a lamb. Blessed souls in Purgatory, how could he have done it? Our father was not a thief, he was a devout man, always gay and so light-hearted and teasing that if any of his friends were feeling depressed they would come to visit him.'

Thinking of her dead father, her expression softened. But then a horrendous cloud darkened her mind, and her whole face wrinkled up with horror at a new thought.

'Supposing that merry old man, that saintly old man, had also committed some crime!'

She no longer trusted anyone, living or dead, old or young. She went to the sick man and he, his face furrowed with pain, his eyes that seemed to beg death to spare him, filled her with infinite tenderness and a nameless grief. As he lay doubled up on the vast bed, he seemed more than ever her little brother. All objects, all people, even the holy dead and the innocent children, now roused hideous doubts, bitter distrust, profound rancour in her mind, while he alone touched her pity, her tenderness, and her love. She must watch him die, indeed, long for death for him. As she nursed him tenderly all she could wish for was that the medicines, the remedies, would be useless. Moreover, this terrible death that she must desire for her 'little brother' was to bring another, still greater pain – the denunciation of the crime. What pained Anna-Rosa above all was that the sick man knew of her anguish.

On the third day of the illness, Isidoro appeared looking very mysterious, carrying a potion prepared by the sacristan. This potion was composed of olive oil, in which floated three scorpions, a centipede, a tarantula, a spider, and a poisonous toadstool. It was said to cure any bite. Anna-Rosa at once smeared it on the sick man's swollen purple hand while Giacobbe asked her calmly, 'Why are you trying to cure me, Anna-Ro? Don't you want me to die?'

She felt as if her heart would break.

'Let it be,' said Giacobbe, looking at Isidoro. 'But if I don't die, what will you do?'

'God will think of something. Don't worry.'

Giacobbe was silent for a moment, then he said, 'Will you go to the judge together?'

'What?'

'To the judge. It's cold now, and it's a long way. You mustn't go on horseback, Anna-Rosa, you know. You must go to Nuoro in a carriage.'

'Why?' she asked, irritably.

'To see the judge, of course.'

She scolded him, then she went into the kitchen and wept bitterly.

'Look, here's your oil,' she said to Isidoro, as he was leaving. 'You could at least take it away. When is Father Elias coming?'

'He's coming this evening.'

'Giacobbe must confess. Time is flying, he's very ill. He didn't sleep a wink last night. He's like a wounded bird.'

'Have the Dejas been?'

'They've been. Mother and son. Brontu came twice. Yes, yes, they're all coming, but what's the use? No one can grant life or death.'

'There is good and bad in him,' said Isidoro, carefully wrapping his red handkerchief round the bottle of oil.

'And in everyone,' replied the woman.

Shortly afterwards the doctor arrived. He was already drunk, and he belched and spat sometimes even over himself. Fumes of grappa came from his purple lips. He was most alarmed at Giacobbe's condition.

'What the hell's wrong with you? Your side? Your side? What the hell, your side? Let's see a moment.'

He lifted the blankets, uncovered Giacobbe's hairy side, prodded it, and put his ear to it.

'The bastard. You're like a spoiled child,' he said, covering him again untidily. But when Anna-Rosa accompanied him to the door, he turned and stared at her.

'Woman,' he said, 'have him confess himself – he may have pneumonia.'

At dusk Giacobbe confessed. Then he sent his sister off saying, 'Anna-Ro, Father Elias will go with you to the judge. Go in a carriage, because it's cold.'

Outside it was snowing, and a profoundly sad, white glow penetrated the large mysterious room whose ceiling was like a cloud-laden sky. Father Elias looked at Anna-Rosa, of whom he

135

was very fond, because she was so like his mother. She seemed to have shrunk still smaller, black in the dismal darkness of the snowy twilight, and she wrinkled up her face in grief at her brother's crime. Father Elias could imagine the conflicts in her poor soul, and he prayed for her silently.

XV

It was May. The great valley of the Isalle, usually so sombre, was now decked with tall grass, flowering shrubs, and fields of barley that waved in the breeze. The clear trilling of the nightingales pierced the vast silence of the valley like the notes of a flute. Great flowering thickets of narcissus and broom massed on the hill-slopes, as if intent on watching the valley floor.

The sun had just set, and in the west the sky was the colour of a ripe peach, while to the north and east the mountains reared up like huge precious stones on a lilac background.

Costantino Ledda had been released from prison a few hours earlier in Nuoro. Now he was on his way home, on foot, slowly descending into the valley, a small bundle on his shoulders. Sometimes he stopped and glanced this way and that along the path. 'The valley seems smaller,' he thought. 'It must be because I've seen the sea.'

He had aged and was clean-shaven and pale but without the tragic look he had once worn. He was alone and on foot, because he had no way of knowing the exact day of his release, otherwise some relatives or friends would certainly have come to meet him. A keen impatience to see the village urged him on. Perhaps because at Nuoro he had been given a bottle of good wine, he was almost cheerful. As he descended, his legs sometimes gave way, but he was not put out by so small a thing.

'When I can't go any further,' he thought, 'I'll lie down and sleep. I have bread and wine in my bundle. What more do I need? I am free as a bird. Once I had a wife, but now I'm a bachelor.'

He thought he was laughing but his lips did not move. Down he went, now intent on the path edged by tall grass, now watching the birds that flew low, almost brushing the earth, pacing themselves against his stride, then flying back into the scrub to sleep. He remembered the old magpie in the prison, and something melted in his heart. He had felt pain at leaving the prison, those companions he did not love, those dismal walls, that sky like a metal sheet hung over the prison yard that had oppressed him for so many years.

After the death of the real murderer, days and months had passed before the law had gone through all the formalities necessary to free the innocent man. To Costantino, who had been told of all that had happened, the days seemed like years. On leaving, he had almost wept.

Now that sorrow too had passed. Everything had passed, as also had the great pain of Giovanna's treachery. He almost felt he could laugh about it.

He reached the bottom of the valley and began to walk along the bank of the Isalle. The sunset light was still brilliant, and water shone here and there between oleanders and rushes, reflecting the red-gold glare of the sky. The lacy umbrellas of elder and the bright coral buds of the oleanders stood out against the light sky as if set in silver enamel-work. Tired by now, Costantino began to realize that the valley was not as small as it had seemed when he had first seen it again.

'I'll sleep well in the open air,' he thought. Sitting down at the edge of a wheatfield, Costantino took from his little bundle a dry gourd full of wine, and drank, drenching his face. He put the gourd back and looked at the field. It was as if he were on the edge of a lake, on which emeralds floated over the scrub, red with the blood of poppies.

Calmer now, he continued his journey, but he no longer walked with his previous eagerness. Whether he got there that day or the next it came to the same thing, since no one was expecting him. The first evening shadows began to close in on him before he reached the end of the valley. The crickets seemed to saw the grass with little silver sickles, the scent of the flowers and the greenery hung warmly on the air, the breeze had spent itself, the birds were silent, and only the black triangles of the bats furrowed the luminous dusk.

Costantino walked on. After long years of brutal oppression, passed between ugly walls, among corrupt men, where the air itself was imprisoned, he was crossing open spaces, tramping over grass and rocks, and as he climbed the mountains that surged up from the valleys he saw the horizon open up more and more and the sky spread out, infinite and gentle as liberty itself, but never in prison had he experienced the intense sadness that filled him as the darkness fell from this free sky. Why was he walking? Where was he walking to? He had been light-hearted at the beginning of his journey, he had seemed to be heading for a place where he had found a little joy. Now he could not at all understand the way he had felt. In the inconclusive dusk that hid the distances, his journey seemed pointless. No longer had he homeland, home, nor family. He would never arrive at any destination. He felt as if he were lost in an endless ashy waste, like the sky spread over his head, in which stars twinkled like the fires of solitary wayfarers, each unknown to the next, lost as he was in the empty freedom of a desert.

He did not sadden himself by thinking of Giovanna, of his lost happiness, of the misery that unjust fate had sent him. Those sorrows had so marked the very core of his being that he seemed to have forgotten them, as one forgets the jacket one has put on. But there was a faint regret still for material things he had lost and would never regain.

He remembered with intensity the yard in front of Giovanna's house, the stones of the little wall where they used to sit together on summer evenings, and above all he remembered the high, wide bed where he used to lie beside her after the weary day. Now it was as if he was returning, tired after one of those long days, but he no longer had anywhere to go home to and rest.

Reaching the top of a slope, he sat down and opened his pack. Night had fallen, clear and diaphanous. To the east, between the mountains that hid the sea, the sky paled in the limpid light of the moon's dawn. The Milky Way lay across it like a deserted white street. In the strange light the scrub looked like a flock of black sheep, and the vast silence was disturbed only by the prolonged sob of the cuckoo.

Costantino ate and drank, then he lay on his back on the brow of the hill and for a moment contemplated the deep solitude of the bright street that furrowed the sky. Then he closed his eyes and, feeling the benefit of the food, the wine, and the rest, grew once more as happy as when he started his journey.

Hardly had he sunk into sleep when he saw his companions in the gaol and he seemed, in his dreams, to be working at the cobbler's bench. He felt a childish pleasure at all the experiences he would relate to his friends in Orlei. He must get up, set off again, get there soon.

But he did not move. Confused images passed through his mind. The King of Spades, seated on a donkey, was riding along the Milky Way. He called to Costantino two or three times. Costantino opened one sleepy eye, closed it, and opened it again. 'Fool, it's the cuckoo,' he thought. 'I'm going to get up now. I must get up.' And he fell asleep.

When he awoke the moon was high in the sky and the dew was falling in the bluish light. Thick shadows like black garments lay draped over the mountain flanks, but every rock, every shrub, every flower stood out clearly on the ground where the moon shone. The cuckoo's high metallic call pierced the night.

Costantino was cold, the dew had soaked him. He got up and gave a prolonged yawn that resounded in the great silence. Then he looked at the sky to guess the time. The morning star had not yet appeared above the horizon. Dawn, then, was a long way away and Costantino set off again, hoping to reach the village before anyone awoke.

He did not want to expose himself to public curiosity and feared, above all, to be seen by Giovanna or her mother, wishing neither to see them nor to pass by their house. Everything was over. After years of suffering, after a thousand schemes for revenge, he now felt he despised Giovanna, and he too wanted to begin a new life.

140

He clambered over hillocks lit up by the moon, where the rock-rose bushes and the asphodel bathed in dew, and the rocks themselves gave out a clammy scent. Threads of water trickled down among the flowering pennyroyal.

His mind was drowsy, but his limbs were agile and fresh. Sometimes he leapt from rock to rock, scrambling up steep short cuts and then he stopped, high on the mountainside, panting, his heart beating hard. The moon threw shimmering silver into his clear eyes.

The further he went, the more well-known landmarks he could pick out, and he smelled in the air the wild fragrance of his native land. He recognized the melancholy tracts where the barley and wheat shoots were still young and green, the mastic scrub, the sparse trees murmuring at each gust of wind like old people talking in their sleep, and farther on still the blade of the sea – that sea that he felt proud to have sailed, no matter in what way. When he reached the church of St Francis he paused again, took off his hat and prayed, and as he prayed, for the first time the keen joy of returning home swept over him.

The sky was just beginning to pale when Isidoro heard a knocking at his door. For two or three weeks, indeed for months and months, he had been waiting for that sound, and now he leaped to his feet, even before joy set his old heart dancing in his breast. The door opened. He saw a tall man with a long pale face wearing, instead of the local costume, a coarse cotton suit, tough as leather. At first Isidoro did not know who it was.

Costantino burst out laughing, a harsh laugh that hurt the fisherman. Then Isidoro recognized his young friend, and a cold shiver went through him. It was indeed Costantino, but not the Costantino of bygone days. All the same, he embraced the young man without kissing him, and his heart melted with emotion.

'You didn't recognize me,' said Costantino, slipping his bundle off his shoulders. 'I knew you.'

His voice and his accent had changed. After the cold fear and the pity, Isidoro felt unease.

'Why are you dressed like that? You could have waited in Nuoro. I'd have brought you clothes and a horse too. Did you come on foot?'

'No, St Francis lent me his horse. Well, what have you got, Isidoro? I don't want coffee. Have you any grappa?'

The fisherman, who was stoking up the fire, turned round, upset at not being able to offer the other man a little coffee.

'I don't know,' he said, spreading his hands, 'but wait, I'll go at once. I was expecting you and not expecting you, and I was about to go out.'

'Where to?' cried the other man, grabbing him. 'I don't want anything. I was joking. Sit down here.'

Isidoro sat down and glanced timidly at Costantino, then little by little he plucked up courage, patted the young man's trousers and knees, and asked if he was going to stay dressed like that. Through the wide-open door the dawn light entered, and Costantino's face looked grey and defeated.

'I'll stay dressed like this, yes,' he said, and again laughed that evil-sounding laugh. 'I'll be leaving so soon.'

'Must you go? Where to?'

'I have met so many people,' began Costantino, as if reciting a lesson. 'People who'll help me. What am I going to do here?'

'You could be a cobbler. Didn't you write to me that you wanted to be a cobbler? You could make a lot of money.'

'I know a police inspector called Burrai' – for Costantino the King of Spades was always a police inspector – 'who lives in Rome, and he's written to me. He's going to get me a post as a cobbler in the king's palace.'

Isidoro looked at him with pitying eyes. How the poor man had changed. 'Why is he talking nonsense like this when we have deep and bloody things to talk of?' he wondered. It seemed to him that Costantino was pretending, that he had wrapped himself in a cloak of feigned indifference. But why? If he did not open up to Isidoro, to whom would he open up?

'Let's talk now, Costantino. Why don't you want any coffee? It'll do you good.'

'Say what you want then,' said Costantino in his flat voice. 'I know you're surprised I don't burst into tears. I've wept so much I don't want to any more. Anyway, I'm going away. I can't stay here now I've crossed the sea. All right, give me some coffee. Who's that going by?' he said, starting up at the sound of footsteps outside. 'I don't want anyone to see me.' He got up and closed the door.

When he returned his face had changed and his chin was quivering. He said softly, 'I went past *there*, on my way here. I didn't want to go that way but I found myself there without wishing it. How can I possibly stay here? Tell me!'

He put his hand to his face and shook his head desperately. Then he threw himself down, writhing and weeping with stifled cries of indescribable violence, like a roped bull marked by the branding iron. The fisherman blenched but said nothing to quieten this storm of grief. At last he recognized his Costantino.

XVI

As soon as the news of Costantino's return spread, the fisherman's hovel filled with people, and all day friends and relatives came and went and people who had never before exchanged a word with the ex-convict now came, embraced him, and offered him their homes. The women wept, calling him 'my son', and watched him with pitying eyes. A neighbour sent bread and sausage. At length, this show of respect and sympathy began to annoy the young man.

'Why are they being so sympathetic to me?' he said to Isidoro. 'Throw them out. Let's go off into the fields.'

'We'll go, we'll go, Son of God, be patient,' replied the old man, leaning over the fire to cook the sausage.

'How wicked you've become. I can hardly believe it.'

After Costantino's fit of grief, Isidoro was no longer suspicious of the young man. He began to take liberties, scolding him as if he were a child. In the few minutes they had been alone he had started to tell the whole story of the events in the village. Costantino listened eagerly and became restless when visitors arrived and interrupted the tale.

The mayor with the Napoleonic face came, and his visit really moved Costantino.

'We'll give you sheep and cows,' said the mayor, blowing his nose with his fingers. 'Every shepherd will give you one beast. If you need anything, tell me immediately. We're all brothers in this world, but particularly in the small villages.'

Costantino thought of what his brothers in the village had done to him, and he shook his head. 'My brothers did to me what Cain did to Abel. There are not enough cows or sheep to console me for my loss.'

'No matter,' said the mayor, carried away by his idea. 'Now that you've travelled, tell me, did you ever look down from a high mountain on to the villages scattered over the country-side below? Didn't it seem to you as if each of those villages was one house, where lived one single family?'

Costantino, wearied of this talk, replied that he had to leave the village, to go away, far away, and never return.

'You're not going away? No, you mustn't go away,' ordered the mayor. 'Where will you go? You must stay here, where we're all brothers.'

Dr Puddu came carrying a large dirty grey umbrella and went over to see what was in the cooking pot.

'The reason you're such a delinquent is because you're only eating pig swill,' he bawled in his harsh voice, tapping the pot with his umbrella.

'Don't break it,' said Isidoro, 'and excuse me, but that's not pig swill. It's beans and bacon and sausage.'

'And doesn't the bacon come from pig? You're all pigs here. So you've come back, you rascal? I watched him die. Who? Who? Giacobbe Dejas, of course. He died a bad death, as he deserved. You should take a purge tomorrow. After a journey it's absolutely essential.'

Costantino looked at him silently.

'You think I'm mad,' shouted the doctor, threatening with his umbrella. 'A purge, understand, a purge.'

'I heard,' said Costantino.

'That's better. I also heard that you're going away. Away. Go to the devil, but go away. But before you go, drop by on that dung heap you call the churchyard. And if you scrabble like a dog you can gnaw the bones of Giacobbe Dejas.'

He ground his teeth as if gnawing a bone. Costantino turned to look at him in amazement.

'Why are you staring at me like that? You've always been a fool, my dear boy, a little animal. Look at old Isidoro over there, calm and serene as the Pope. They've taken everything from you, even against the law, and you don't even know what

145

it's worth. They've betrayed you, killed you, they've beaten you cruelly, and you stand there stupidly like a child. Why don't you do something? Why don't you go to that wicked woman's house and her mother's and her mother-in-law's and take them by the hair and tie them to the tails of those cows they want to give you to soothe you, and set fire to their skirts and then chase the cows out into the town so that they set fire to everything? Do you understand? Do you understand, fool?'

He shouted in their faces, breathing foul fumes of absinthe over them, his eyes bloodshot. Costantino backed away, shaken by the doctor's words. He could not control the feeling that the horrible man was right. The doctor got up to leave and, turning in the doorway to shake his umbrella, he yelled, 'You make me want to break this over your head. Men like you deserve what they get. At least take the purge, idiot.'

'That I will do,' said Costantino. He laughed, but the doctor's words left him deeply disturbed. Sometimes he was seized by a terrible fit of despair. He wanted to leave but he did not know exactly where to go, nor did he know what he could do if he stayed in the village.

I have no home. Today they come to greet me, out of curiosity, but tomorrow no one will remember me. I'm like a bird without a nest. What shall I do? What use is the law? Perhaps my indifference may be the worst punishment for that woman? Nevertheless, the doctor's words echoed in his mind. Ought he to go to that house and, like a bolt of lightning, destroy those who had destroyed his life?

'No, Costantino, she is not happy,' went on Isidoro as they ate the sausage and white bread that the neighbour had sent as a present. 'She isn't happy. I never look her straight in the face nowadays, and when I see her I have the strange feeling that I'm looking at the devil. But I'm sorry for her. She has a daughter who, they tell me, is as puny and green as a beanshoot. How can the child of mortal sin be beautiful? The baby was baptized like a bastard. The priest did not even go back to the house, and the people sneered in the streets.'

'Do you remember my baby?' asked Costantino, slicing the

thick, rancid bacon. 'He wasn't like a beanshoot. If only he had lived!'

'It's better that he is dead,' the fisherman said philosophically. 'Life is full of misery. It is better to die innocent and to go away up there into paradise beyond the clouds, beyond all human misery. Drink, Costantino,' he went on. 'This wine isn't much good, but it's not quite vinegar yet. I remember last year, on the Feast of the Assumption, Giacobbe Dejas invited me to have supper with him. He was afraid of me. He thought I knew about him, and he wanted me to marry his sister. If you could have seen the woman you wouldn't laugh. She went with me and the priest to Nuoro to see the judge. Thus God helped me in the hour of death, for I have never seen a braver woman. Afterwards she became bent and shrivelled, like those fruits that wither on the plant before they ripen. I often go to visit her; to cheer her up, I say "Well, are we going to get married, my barley grain?" We both smile, though really we want to weep. Giacobbe seemed happy and content. He was getting rich, he was thinking of marrying. Then all at once, boom. He dropped like a rotten pear. That's life. Bachisia Era bartered her daughter, thinking she'd change her own life, and now she's the one who's going to die of starvation first. Giovanna Era did what she did, thinking she'd find heaven on earth, and instead she finds herself like a skewered frog on a stick.'

'Does he beat her?' asked Costantino, grieved.

'He doesn't beat her, but there are worse things than beatings. They've made her into a servant, you know, a slave even. You know how the ancient folk treated their slaves? That's how she's treated in that house.'

'God rot them. Let's drink to their damnation,' said Costantino, lifting his glass.

Hearing that Giovanna was unhappy, he felt a cruel joy, a sensation of luxurious delight.

After their meal, the two men went and lay down in the shade of a wild fig tree. It was a hot afternoon. The still air smelled of poppies, the horizon shimmered in an ashy vapour, and the bees buzzed. Tired and defeated, Costantino slept at once, but the fisherman could not close his eyes. A grasshopper

147

leapt over the grass and on to the poppies, and Isidoro stretched out an arm to catch it.

I know why he wants to go away. He still loves her, poor boy. If he stays here he'll suffer like St Lawrence on the gridiron. Look at him, poor fellow. He looks like a sick child. What have they done to him? They've torn him apart as they'd tear a grasshopper.

A shadow appeared at the end of the path, and Isidoro recognized Father Elias. He got up and went to meet him and lead him into the hovel, trying not to awaken Costantino. But Costantino slept lightly; he awoke, and heard someone talking about him.

'It would be better if he left,' said the priest in a grave voice. 'Much better.'

But Costantino did not leave. Days went by, the people stopped pestering him, and he was able to move around the village without being an object of curiosity to anyone.

With the money he had earned in prison he bought leather and soles and thread, but he did not start to work. Every day he bought meat, fruit, and wine, and he ate and drank a lot, pretending that Isidoro was doing likewise. The fisherman's hospitality weighed on him, he was afraid that the village people might think he was scrounging, and he made a point of being generous to Isidoro and to everyone else. He took crowds of acquaintances to the tavern where they all got drunk, and he would tell the story of his life in prison with a great deal of embellishment and exaggeration. His money soon went, and when Isidoro scolded him he said, 'Well, I have no children, I have no one to think of. Leave me alone.' He was expecting a legacy from his murdered uncle, a legacy that his relatives had promised to restore to him without recourse to law. 'Then I'll sell everything and go away,' he said. 'I'll give you a hundred *scudi*, Isidoro.'

The poor fisherman wanted nothing. He only wanted Costantino to be as he used to be before the disaster – good, industrious, and not false. The old man sensed that the young man was putting on an act and he was deeply grieved. Often he caught Costantino with tear-filled eyes, and then Isidoro's old heart leapt in joy.

'What's the matter, son?' he would ask. But Costantino would laugh as the tears coursed down his cheeks.

Sometimes they went leech-fishing together, and, while Isidoro stood with his bare legs immersed in stagnant water at a place where the brook was still, Costantino lay in the rushes, told stories, and gazed at the horizon with a strange nostalgia.

He had wanted to go away, because up there, under that fateful sky, in the dead solitude of the high plain, guarded by the huge mountain sphinxes, he felt as if he were being throttled by a red-hot iron hoop. Everything from the blades of grass that grew in the byways to the mountain peaks reminded him of the past. Every night he circled, sly as a fox, round Giovanna's house. One evening he saw the tall figure of the young woman leave the portico and go across to *their* house. It was the first time he had seen Giovanna. He recognized her despite the damp darkness of a rather cloudy evening. His heart beat violently, and each beat sent forth a different pain, a memory, a spasm of despair. He was on the point of throwing himself at the woman, embracing her, killing her. He could not bear this lurking in the darkness to catch a glimpse of her. He was seized with the desire to go up to her in broad daylight, but she never came out, and in the daytime he was afraid of approaching the white house.

One Saturday evening he heard Brontu's laugh coming from the portico, and he thought he heard her laugh too. His eyes filled and a pain shot through him. But he went on pretending he did not care, while everyone in Orlei seemed hostile to him. Everyone – even Isidoro. Sometimes he wondered in a baffled way why he had even come back. He had returned because he could not live anywhere else but in the infinite calm of the high plain, limited only by the empty horizon, where the wild woods of arbutus stretched like a green cloud.

'I'm leaving,' he said to Isidoro. 'I've written to my friend, Burrai. He can do anything, you know. Even if I'd been guilty he'd have got me a pardon from the king.'

'You've already told me that,' replied Isidoro one day, as he

149

stood with his skinny old legs in the brackish water. 'I'm tired of hearing it. Anyway, he hasn't replied yet.'

'He's trying to find me a job. Tell me the truth. Why does the priest want me to go? Is he afraid I'll kill Brontu Dejas?'

'Yes, exactly that.'

'It can't be that. I told him if I'd wanted to kill someone I'd have done so straight away. He kept saying, "Go away, go away, it's better." What do you say, fisherman? Should I leave or not?'

'I've no idea,' said Isidoro. 'All I know is you're like a lazy dog. Why aren't you working, tell me? Why are you going on about this Burrai of yours, you rascal. He's not sparing a thought for you, by the way.'

'Oh, he isn't thinking about me, isn't he?' said Costantino, offended. 'I'll show you whether or not he's thinking of me. Look at this.'

He got up, pulled a letter out of his inner jacket pocket, and began to read it. It was from Burrai, in Rome, where he had set himself up in a little shop selling Sardinian wines. Of course, he exaggerated the size of the business, saying he was the owner of a large wine store. He offered Costantino his hospitality, told him off for not coming to Rome, and assured him of work. The fisherman's blue eyes widened in childlike amazement.

'Well, well,' he remarked. 'Why didn't you say so earlier? Why did you hide the letter? How much does it cost to go to Rome?'

'Fifty *lire*, that's all.'

'Have you got it?'

'Of course.'

'Then go, go!' exclaimed the old man, stretching his hand out towards the horizon.

He was silent a moment. He leaned over and stared at the bottom of the stream, at the pebbles like large white eggs, while Costantino gazed indifferently ahead. Beside the stream the breeze bent the high golden grass. Long oat stalks shook against the blue background, as if in a veil of water. Isidoro realized the time had come to explain to Costantino why many people wanted him to leave the town.

150

'Giovanna doesn't love her husband. You and she might meet again.'

'What if we do?'

'Nothing. It could happen, that's all.'

'What of it?' cried Costantino, his voice ringing out strongly on the quiet river bank. 'I despise the filthy woman. I don't want her. I could kill her or have her put in gaol with her idiot lover, but I despise them so much I don't care.'

'You don't love her? That's why you buzz round her house like a fly round a honeypot?'

'So you know about that,' said Costantino guiltily. 'It's not true – well, yes, it's true. I buzz round her house. So what?'

'Nothing. You must leave.'

'I'm leaving. Am I a burden on you?'

'Costantino! Costantino!' cried the old man in a heartbroken voice.

Costantino wrenched the heads off a handful of rushes, threw them away, and went back to gazing into the distance. His expression changed, just as it had the day he came back, after he had closed Isidoro's door behind him. The dimple on his chin quivered. Several times he swallowed the bitter saliva that filled his mouth, then he said, 'Why does the priest want me to leave? Aren't I Giovanna's real husband? Supposing she does come back to me! Aren't I her real husband?'

'If she comes back to you, my son, Brontu Dejas will really kill you. He's not one to go to church to pray.'

'I'm not afraid. I don't want her. She's a fallen woman in my eyes. I'm going a long way away. I'm going to marry another woman. Wait until the divorce law comes and then you'll see.'

'You won't do that, you're a good Christian,' murmured the old man in a caressing voice.

'I won't do that,' repeated Costantino, as if hypnotized by the caressing voice.

'You won't do that, you won't do it, you're a good Christian,' repeated the old man, and his voice grew sad, remembering past experiences and the ways of the world. He murmured to himself, 'If he doesn't, it isn't only because he's a good Christian.'

151

XVII

As the July evening fell serenely, Costantino sat on the stone bench outside the fisherman's house, counting on his fingers. He had been back for sixty-four days. Sixty-four days. It seemed like yesterday. It seemed like a century. His coarse cotton suit was now threadbare, his face had bronzed, and his heart, corroded from day to day, hour to hour, by grief, bitterness, and passion, had darkened as if in the grip of corruption.

From prison he had brought with him the habit of pretence. He did not know why, but he could not manage to trust anyone, even though he felt the need, and this pretence increased his sorrow. An endless cold emptiness surrounded him, like the calm limitless sea around a shipwreck. For two months he had been swimming in this sea, and now he was tired, devoid of strength. However much he stared into desolate distances, he could not perceive the shore, he could not see any end to his pointless struggle. The cold water and the abyss of emptiness were slowly engulfing him.

Every day he spoke of going, yet still he did not leave. It was a pretence, like everything else. He felt that he would never leave. Why should he go? Here or there, life was the same. He loved no one, he hated no one, he felt as if he had become as hideous as the prisoners he had left behind. Isidoro, for whom he had felt a lively affection when he was far away, was nothing to him now, close up, and sometimes the old man annoyed him. When Isidoro was away, occupied with his fishing or travelling to sell the ropes he made, Costantino felt freed from a burden. The old man's paternal watchfulness irritated and intimidated him.

That evening the fisherman was away, and Costantino immediately felt a sense of freedom. Now he could do what he pleased, without feeling preached at by anyone, without feeling that instinctive fear and irritation that he remembered from his prison life and that the presence of the old man used to re-create. Costantino was waiting for a woman. He despised women now, and felt truly disgusted in their company, but he had embarked on a light relationship with a half-idiot girl who lived not far from Giovanna's house and who one night, surprising him near the Dejas' portico, had taken him into her home.

She had told him all the gossip about the Dejas household, and he went to her every time he was spotted near the white house. Sometimes he made her come to Isidoro's house when the old man was out, but he despised her and treated her strangely. That evening when she arrived he did not stir from the stone bench but told her to sit beside him.

'It's hot inside. There are fleas, spiders and devils. Stay out here in the fresh air,' he said, without looking at her.

'But they'll see us,' she replied, in a loud coarse voice.

'Let them see us. I don't care, and what difference does it make to you?'

'It matters a lot to me, in fact.'

'What does it matter if men see you?' he said, raising his voice. 'They're all sinners themselves. And God can see inside just as well as out.'

'Let's go in, you've been drinking,' she said without annoyance, and she went into the cottage. She lit the lamp, looked into the store cupboard and, as Costantino did not come in, she went to the door and said, 'If you don't come in, I'm leaving. I've something to tell you.'

He sprang up, came in, and began to embrace her, while she burst into crazy laughter.

'Oh, there you are. That made you jump to it, my little shorn lamb.'

She was tall and plump, with a small head, a tiny brown face, a red mouth, and green eyes. Though not ugly, her appearance was nevertheless repugnant. She never drank, but she always seemed tipsy and was convinced that everyone else was too. She went on laughing and searching in the store cupboard.

'There's nothing here,' she said. 'Absolutely nothing. I'm hungry, you know.'

'If you wait a moment I'll get you something. But you've got to tell me first.'

She turned to him and pushed at his chest with one hand while slapping him quite hard with the other. 'Oh, so you want to know, you monster. You want to know, do you? That's why you came in so quickly. Go back outside, you shorn lamb. You want to know. You think it's about Giovanna Era, eh? And you came in because of that, not because of me.'

'Leave me alone,' he said, grabbing her hand. 'You're hitting me too hard. Yes, that's what I came in for. So?'

'I'm not going to tell you anything.'

'Mattea, don't make me angry,' he said gently. 'You're not a bad woman. I'll buy you whatever you want this minute. What do you want to eat? What?'

He was like a child, pretending to be good to get what he wanted. He desperately wanted something harsh and brutal just then. He wanted news that Brontu had beaten Giovanna, or that something bad had happened to her, or that serious disaster had befallen the Dejas household. He was therefore hardly delighted when Mattea said with a wink, 'Somebody stole some cattle from them. As soon as they found out the old woman rushed off like a mad thing to see what the damage was. She's going to spend the night in the sheepfold, and his wife is all alone. Do you understand, all alone?'

'What do I care?' he said. But he felt the blood sing in his ears at the thought that Giovanna herself might have sent Mattea.

'Fool, you could go to her house. Aren't you going, then? I came to tell you. Go on, do me a favour; I'm sorry for you. After all, you're her husband.'

'I'm not married to anyone,' he said, shrugging his shoulders. 'I thought you were going to tell me something quite different. So what do you want me to buy? Beans, milk, bacon, cherries?'

'Marry me, then, if you're not married to anyone,' said Mattea in her rough, shaky, drunkard's voice.

Costantino cleared his throat and spat. Her usually vague eyes took on a gleam of intelligence. She wrinkled her forehead.

'Why are you spitting?' she asked. 'Is Giovanna better than me perhaps?'

He blushed and then a sadness came over his heart. 'You!' he said. 'You may be better or you may be worse.'

'What?'

'If you're not lying at this moment, if you didn't come to harm me by telling me she is alone, then you're better than she.'

'Why should I want to harm you? I'm sorry for you. I swear on the memory of the departed dead that if you go to her tonight you'll run no risk.'

'How can I believe you, woman? You don't even have respect for the dead.'

Mattea got up to leave, offended and indignant. He stopped her.

'Filthy dog,' she said scornfully. 'I was sorry for you, and you're rude to me. What have I done to you? What?'

She raised her head proudly, showing her creased forehead. Her eyes were newly full of intelligence. He looked at her, astonished that such a woman could speak in such a way, that she could raise her head and look at him so proudly. Then he burst out laughing.

'I'm going now,' he repeated. 'I'll go and come back at once. I'll bring wine too, even if you don't drink. Wait for me. Wait for me,' he ordered sharply, for Mattea was following him. 'And don't pester me.'

She stopped at the door. He went out but had only taken a few steps when he heard her coarse voice calling him back. He went back to the door and through the crack of light he saw Mattea's nose and one of her eyes grown stupid again.

'What do you want, you cross-eyed goat?'

'If you're going to her, don't expect me to wait here.'

'To hell with what you do!' swore Costantino. 'I'll think of going to her when you think of going to church.'

When he returned a few minutes later, the strange girl had

vanished. He thought she was hiding, and he hunted for her, calling her in a low voice, saying he had bought bread, meat, and fruit, but she had gone. Total silence reigned in the little house. Only the fig leaves rustled mysteriously, black against the colourless sky.

Costantino was annoyed by Mattea's disappearance. What was he to do for the rest of the night? He was not sleepy. He had slept during the afternoon, and he did not know where to go. He ate and drank, and from time to time he spoke to himself out loud.

'If she thinks I'm going to her house she's got another think coming.'

Then: 'Innocent as a new-born lamb! She's crazy.'

Then: 'Mattea gives me the creeps. She's like an animal.'

Then he swore. Then he laughed, in the light, vague laugh he used when he was alone. He drank all the while in big gulps, and every time he emptied his glass he sighed and wiped his hands on his chest. He felt almost happy.

'To hell with her! To the devil with her!' He went out, lay down on the stone bench and gave himself up to his real thoughts: 'She's alone. Well, so what? I despise her, and I wouldn't go to her house if she told me it was full of gold. What would I do with gold?' He asked himself this sadly but then he began to sing softly.

'Dear little heart, beloved heart
I wait and days pass by.
When you come the kite will soar,
Weaving in the sky.'

For a while his low, toneless singing distracted him, but then his thoughts took their course again: 'If I do go, what will happen? Aren't I her husband? But I can't go there. Fool! Isidoro makes me laugh, the old fool. Go away, he says, or Brontu Dejas might kill you because he doesn't go to church or confession.'

He began to sing again. The harsh rustle of the fig leaves accompanied his voice.

156

'When you see the grapevine,
It will flower in June.
Then you'll see the swineherd
Fattening pigs for brawn.'

He shifted and closed his eyes. His head rocked on the palm of the hand which propped it up.

'So. What then?' he said aloud. He opened his eyes wide as if terrified by his own voice, closed them again, and spoke softly to himself. 'No, I don't want her as my wife any more. She's a fallen woman. She's been with another man, and as she's been with him she could come back to me or could go with others. She's like Mattea – I spit in her face.'

He opened his eyes again and spat with scorn for Giovanna. Then, tender memories of times long gone passed through his mind. He remembered one morning when he had awakened his wife with a kiss. Opening her eyes briefly, rather surprised, she had said, 'I thought you were someone else.'

Was it an accident he had remembered that? He was a fool. He did not even know if Giovanna would welcome him or throw him out should he go to see her. He decided she would not welcome him. He felt that he had to go on living and suffering but that if he went and she did not want him, perhaps a ray of light would be kindled in the cold emptiness that surrounded him. For he still wanted her, still desired her. He had never for one moment ceased to want her, to desire her, but he still dreamed of an honest Giovanna, lost for ever on this earth, but his alone in eternity. If she now deceived her second husband too, even for the first, she would not be honest. In the secret depths of his conscience he considered Brontu Dejas to be Giovanna's real husband.

It was about ten o'clock, and he was still lying on the little bench when a melancholy tune floated through the air. It was the blind boy playing the accordion in the distance and singing a deep, monotonous, sad song. The song seemed to express an overwhelming nostalgia, as if the dead were remembering the few happy days of their lives. The music especially seemed to beg for light, joy, happiness – all the

157

things that the dead had left and would never have again. Costantino shivered and stood up. The song and the music retreated further and further into the distance and then ceased.

Costantino felt a wave of tenderness and anguish wash over his heart. In the darkness, in the infinite silence, in the vast solitude that surrounded him, he understood that overwhelming need of the blind man for the light. He felt like a sleepwalker. He could hear, under his feet, the rustle of dry leaves that the wind had swept up and piled round Isidoro's cottage. His eyes, accustomed to the darkness, could see the lighter line of the street, the black cottages, the empty background of the horizon. Then he seemed to wake up and to quicken his step.

Here and there, in front of the cottages where the inhabitants were too poor to light a lamp, groups of people sat enjoying the air. He greeted them and passed by. In a deserted corner he saw two lovers, the man trying to hide the woman and she turning her head to the wall. To scare the young people Costantino was tempted to call, 'I'm going to tell your father.' But he was afraid of being spotted himself, and he went on by.

When he reached the black mass of the almond tree that leaned out over the street, his heart began to thump as he approached Bachisia's house. He thought he saw a huge black head with wild hair staring at him in the distance.

He had decided to walk round the other way and to go right into the Dejas' house and see Giovanna. It all seemed easy to him, and he felt ready for anything, although he was afraid. He heard a girl's voice say, 'Whatever you say it's not true.'

He looked round but could see no one. He went on, his anxiety mounting with each step. He crossed the open yard in front of the houses, passed Bachisia's cottage, then the white house, then Mattea's hovel. A small window in the last cottage was lit up. The rest was in darkness. Once again he thought that Mattea must have been acting for Giovanna, but she could have deceived him. Bachisia might be at Giovanna's house or Giovanna might be asleep and not open the door. Without hesitation he went on to the portico. At once he made out the figure of Giovanna seated on the front steps. She too recognized him immediately and jumped to her feet, rigid with terror, but his weary, distressed voice reassured her.

'Don't be afraid. Are you alone?'

'Yes.'

They fell into each other's arms.

XVIII

A year went by. One night, when Brontu was away from home, Martina heard, or thought she heard, a low whispering coming from Giovanna's room.

'Has Brontu got back?' thought the old woman. 'Why has he come back? Has some disaster happened at the sheepfold?'

She was so worried by this thought that she got out of bed. The door was open. She could hear a subdued muttering in Giovanna's room. She did not want to light the lamp, so in the darkness she crossed the room between her bedroom and Giovanna's, but after a few steps she bumped into a chair, which fell over.

'Holy Mary,' groaned the old woman, lifting up the chair. She groped her way to the door and tried to open it. It was locked.

'What do you want?' called out Giovanna.

'Is Brontu back?'

'No. Why?'

'I thought I heard someone talking. Why did you lock the door?'

'Did I lock it? I don't believe I did,' said Giovanna in an innocent voice. 'I'll open it now, wait. I was talking to the baby. She won't go to sleep.'

'Maredda!' The old woman called the baby's name, but the child did not reply. 'Is she asleep now?'

'I'll get up now and open the door,' said Giovanna, in a muffled voice after a moment of silence. The old woman did not reply. At that moment the terrible truth had come to her like a sudden ray of light, and she shuddered. Giovanna must have a lover, and this lover could be none other than

Costantino. In a flash a thousand details to which she had not given a thought, a thousand tiny memories, passed through her mind. Grief and rage shook her, but when Giovanna repeated, 'I'm just coming,' she controlled herself and replied calmly, 'It doesn't matter. Stay in bed.'

Then she went back to her own room again in the dark, saying to herself with fierce calm, 'You must act with great skill here, Martina.'

Her first impulse had been to run outside and see if Giovanna's lover was leaving through the bedroom window that opened on to a lower roof, but she stopped herself, thinking: 'If Giovanna realizes I'm suspicious she'll be on her guard. I must pretend, keep my eyes skinned, find out. And then . . .'

What would happen then? The 'then' was so sad and final that the old woman did not want to think about it. She went back into her room, lay down on the bed, and anguished thoughts crowded into her mind.

What would Brontu have done if he'd known? Poor Brontu. He was a violent man but he was good at heart and loved Giovanna very much. But just because he loved her so much, he might commit a crime to revenge himself if she deceived him.

'It's better he doesn't get to know about this. I hoped to goodness Giovanna would be sensible and not deceive her poor husband. What if I was wrong? What if she was really talking to the baby? No. She had a man in her room and it must have been Costantino. Wretched woman, cursed beggar, is that how you repay those who saved you from starvation, clothed and cared for you? You'll pay for it. We'll chase you away with a whip, naked as you came.'

Martina remembered that she had heard Costantino was on good terms with Giovanna's mother. He had started work some time previously. He had set up a cobbler's shop and earned quite a good living. Could Bachisia know about and be covering up her daughter's affair with her first husband?

'The old witch hates us,' she said to herself, 'and perhaps Costantino gives her presents.'

At dawn she was still awake. She got up, went out and

looked at the wall and the projecting roof over which Giovanna's lover must have climbed down. Then she raised her eyes and saw Giovanna at the window. Suddenly she sensed that the young woman had not slept either, that she too could discern traces of the man who had fled through the window, and that she knew Martina suspected the truth. Across the space that divided them, the two women exchanged a look of bitterness and fear. Martina tried to allay Giovanna's suspicions so as to be able to surprise her with her lover. Giovanna realized her mother-in-law's suspicions, but pretended to have noticed nothing and discreetly continued her relationship with Costantino.

Although Costantino was now working and earning a living, at the bottom of his heart there was still an ineradicable sadness.

'I will do everything I can to force Brontu to throw me out,' Giovanna said to him during their assignations, 'so that he'll suggest a divorce to get free of me. Then I'll come back to you, my love, and we'll never leave each other. I'll be your servant. I'll make you forget all your past sorrows.'

Costantino smiled bitterly. He loved Giovanna, but not as he had during their marriage. He loved her more ardently but less deeply, and he needed her to make him live, but he dared not tell her that if she were to be free again and become his wife once more it would not make him happy. She was no longer his Giovanna. She was another woman, who had deceived her first husband and was now deceiving her second – a woman who belonged to two living men and had deceived them both.

Sometimes he wanted to kill someone, Brontu or Bachisia or Giovanna, to revenge himself for his suffering, but he could not commit a violent act, and he cursed himself for his weakness. His heart was poisoned, and he could no longer feel joy. Isidoro continually advised him to find a wife, even though it was against the old man's own principles.

'I already have a wife,' said Costantino. 'What would I do with another one? She might deceive me too. All woman are the same.'

Isidoro sighed. Daily he feared disaster. He knew, partly by intuition, partly because Costantino had allowed him to guess, that the young man and Giovanna were lovers, and he feared that one day or another there would be a tragedy. So he thought naively that if Costantino had another family, if he had an affectionate, virtuous wife who would give him children, perhaps he would forget and find peace.

But Costantino smiled his usual bitter smile whenever the old fisherman suggested marriage to him.

'You're afraid I'll kill someone, or someone will kill me,' he said. 'Don't worry. Things are going too well for me to think of making new problems for myself.'

The day after Martina had heard the lovers whispering, Costantino appeared, as he often did, at Bachisia's house. He did not like the old witch, who had been the chief instigator of Giovanna's divorce. In those moments when all the bitterness of his sad destiny arose to crush him, the young man felt such hatred against his former mother-in-law that the urge to throttle her raced through his blood like a voluptuous desire. But he went to her house because he needed to relive his past in that cottage where he had been so happy, and because he liked to hear the curses and slanders that Bachisia hurled incessantly at the Dejas.

Did Bachisia know that Giovanna and Costantino were lovers? Neither of them said anything, but, like Isidoro, she had guessed. She was content to let it take its course. Costantino had given her a pair of shoes, and from time to time he did a small service for her. If he had asked her to allow him to meet Giovanna in her house, she would perhaps not have said no, but Costantino had confided nothing to her nor asked for anything. That day he went in cautiously, a little worried, and Bachisia, who was seated by the door spinning, put down her distaff and looked at the young man for a long time, her little eyes full of malice.

Evening fell. Costantino had been working all day. He was tired, unhappy, worried. The sweetness and luminosity of the summer evening, the silence of Bachisia's cottage, the loneliness of the yard in front of the Dejas' house, the warm

163

scent of evening heightened the poignancy of his nostalgia for the past.

He sat on a bench, leaning his elbows on his knees, and his chin on his clasped hands. For a moment neither he nor the old woman spoke. He was thinking of Malthineddu, his dead child. He seemed to see him playing before the door, and he felt the tears trembling in his eyes.

'You know,' Bachisia said suddenly, 'the old nanny-goat is going crazy.'

'Who?' asked Costantino.

'Who? The old miser, Martina Dejas. D'you know what? Last night she got out of bed and went to spy at Giovanna's door. She thought there was a man in there – imagine, my dear. Now she's gone quite crazy – she's always been half-crazy.'

'Ah,' was all Costantino said.

'Listen, my dear,' went on Bachisia, lowering her voice, 'Giovanna says – '

'What?' asked Costantino, lifting his head suddenly.

'She says Martina thinks that you and Giovanna – do you get my meaning? The old hag hasn't said anything, but Giovanna has guessed what she thinks. So – '

'I understand,' said Costantino.

He understood. Giovanna was warning him through Bachisia. He would have to be careful.

'So, my dear,' went on the old woman, 'it would be better if you didn't come here, so as not to make her suspicious. I'll see you like this sometimes at your house, just to chat. Ah,' she sighed, 'you're a real man. Look at you, tall and handsome like a bandit. When I think of that freak of nature Brontu Dejas, and I think of you, I ask myself how Giovanna could have been so wilful as to forget you. Oh, if she'd only listened to me.'

Costantino stood up and the woman's lying words filled him with a fierce desire to hurt someone. 'Shut up!' he said impatiently, but at that moment Bachisia glanced towards the Dejas' house and after a moment murmured, 'See, my dear. We're being spied on. Giovanna is right. Look at the old harpy spying. I'd like to gouge out her eyes.'

Indeed Martina could be seen peering from the dark portico.

At that moment Costantino, who had never really hated Brontu's mother, felt all his anger and resentment turn against Martina. He wanted to hurl himself across the yard, fall upon the old woman, and gouge out her eyeballs.

'Giovanna has told me that she's going to force Dejas to ill-treat her and throw her out of the house,' said Bachisia. 'Then we'll ask for a divorce again. Be careful and patient, my dear. Wait.'

'What have I got to wait for?' he replied in a harsh voice. 'For me, nothing more can happen.'

Bachisia went on talking, but he was no longer listening. He paused on the threshold of what once had been his house. He looked towards the Dejas' portico and felt more and more gloomy. Now his last consolation, having Giovanna as a lover, was about to be taken from him. It was going to be taken away by those who had taken everything from him – everything – and they might also take his life from him if he went on seeing the woman who used to be his wife. All at once he felt such a wave of hatred for the old miser that he wanted to hurl himself into the portico and make the sweet silence ring with the dying Martina's desperate cry. He rushed out of the door and strode quickly towards the Dejas' house. Then he stopped, turned round, and walked away. Bachisia saw him disappear slowly in the soft, silent dusk. From that evening on, he never went back to the old woman's cottage.

One day towards the end of October, Isidoro Pane received an unexpected visit. The old man was seated in front of his hearth, preparing supper for himself and Costantino, who still lived with him. Outside it was already quite cold. Isidoro was thinking of the evening when Giacobbe had been buried in the dung heap to the singing of the widows and young girls. A saucepan was boiling on the hearth and, outside the hovel, the fig tree rustled in the wind with a sad murmur. Someone knocked on the door.

'Who is it?' asked Isidoro.

'*Ave Maria*,' said Martina, entering cautiously, having assured herself that he was alone.

165

'Martina! *Gratia plena*,' replied the old man, surprised to see her.

She was wearing a sort of shawl round her head that hid her face completely. She was paler, sterner than usual, and to Isidoro she seemed to have aged greatly.

'Sit down, Martina Dejas,' he said solicitously, offering her a bench. 'What good wind has brought you to me?'

'I'll wind,' she replied. Then she looked round and said, 'I want to talk to you privately. Can anyone hear us? Where is he?'

'He's still in his workshop. He'll be here later.'

'Look here,' said the old woman, seating herself, 'perhaps you can guess why I've come.'

'I can't guess, Martina Dejas,' he replied, although he knew quite well. 'But why didn't you send for me? I would have come to your house.'

'In my house even the walls have ears. You won't give me away?'

'I won't tell anyone.'

'You're a man of God, Isidoro Pane. You will help me put things right.'

'If I can,' he said, taking her hand. 'Tell me.'

The old woman sighed and said, 'I'll tell you, Isidoro, I'll tell you, although the words I speak will foul my lips. I'll tell you and you alone. A terrible blight has descended on my house. Do you see how I've aged? I haven't closed my eyes for months. Giovanna, my daughter-in-law, has a lover – Costantino Ledda. Aren't you surprised?' she asked, seeing that the old man remained unmoved. 'You already knew about it? Then someone does know. Perhaps lots of people know. Oh, perhaps everyone knows the shame of my house.'

'Don't be afraid, old woman. Calm yourself. Calm. I didn't know, and I don't think anyone knows, and perhaps it isn't true. But if it were known, no one would be surprised.'

'No one would be surprised?'

'Of course not, Martina Dejas. No one. Because they all know that – excuse me for speaking plainly – Giovanna married your son out of self-interest. Costantino has come

166

back. *They* were in love *before*, and if they are in love now, it's natural.'

'It's natural! Why do you say these things, Isidoro Pane? It's natural for a woman to be dishonest? For a beggar picked up in the streets to betray the people who've been so good to her? It's natural for my son, Brontu Dejas, who dared do what no one else dared do, to be betrayed?'

'It's natural.'

'Ah!' exclaimed Martina getting up, her eyes glinting with anger. 'Then it's pointless for me to have come here.'

'Calm down, calm down. Sit down, Martina, and tell me why you came. Let's think of all the aspects of this thing, however useless, and let's be reasonable. I can guess what you wanted to ask me. You want me to persuade Costantino to leave your family alone.'

The old woman sat down again and talked. Yes, she begged Isidoro to talk to Costantino, to advise him to leave Giovanna alone. 'I'll die of the shame,' she finished in a trembling voice. 'But at least my Brontu will not suffer. If he got to know of this, it would destroy him. He'd spill blood, he'd kill Giovanna and Costantino. I keep seeing drops of blood before my eyes. You'll see, Isidoro, you'll see. If we don't find a way to stop this, something terrible will happen.' As she spoke, Martina became even more pale, almost livid. Her lips trembled, her eyes shone with pain and anger.

'You frighten me and you make me feel pity for you,' said Isidoro, in a deep voice. 'But whose fault is it? I remember. Your visit reminds me of another. Giacobbe Dejas. He sat there where you're sitting. He too said we must stop it, we must prevent it; if not, something terrible would happen. We tried to stop it, to prevent it, but we could not. You, your son, you all brought about your own downfall. You fell into mortal sin, you disregarded God's laws, and now your punishment has come.'

'We! Us alone!' said the old woman. 'No, it's everyone's fault. It's Bachisia Era's fault for being greedy and spiteful and pushing her daughter into Brontu's arms. It's Giovanna's fault for deceiving her first husband, while loving him, and giving herself to her second husband out of self-interest. In fact, it's

167

not our fault at all, because we only acted out of good will. It's their fault, theirs alone, and I hate them all, filthy traitors. There'll be terrible trouble if Costantino doesn't stop. Beg him, beseech him. Tell him not to ruin an honourable family. But if he won't listen – '

'Be quiet, Martina,' begged the old man, seeing her great agitation. 'Be quiet and don't talk nonsense. Are you sure Costantino and Giovanna are lovers?'

'I'm sure. I haven't closed my eyes for three months. One night I found out there was someone in Giovanna's room. She realized I was suspicious about something and was cautious for a while. But now it's without restraint, quite open. The other day they met in Bachisia Era's house. I saw them and I heard them. I was listening at the door. Yesterday night he came back to her room, you understand, in my house, under my roof. And I, I, trembling with hate, I waited under the eaves. I wanted to talk to him, hurt him, kill him. I had a knife with me, but I couldn't move. I couldn't open my mouth when he slithered down from the roof like a thief and went off. I'm only a poor old woman. I can't do anything. Giovanna knows I love Brontu more than anything in the world, and to save him I'd sacrifice even the honour of our name. She abused my great love, that ungrateful tramp. She knows I won't say anything to my son, in case he kills her and destroys himself. She takes advantage of me so as to go on deceiving him. If Costantino doesn't stop, there's nothing I won't do. Tell him.'

'Why don't you talk to Giovanna?' asked the old man.

'I'm afraid of her. She's always there in front of me, like a skulking tigress, or rather a tigress lying in wait. She hates me and I hate her. She's waiting for me to say one thing, and then she'll throw me down and strangle me. If I open my mouth, I'm lost. It's terrible, terrible. If you only knew how sad my life is. Death could not be more bitter.'

Martina hid her face in her hands and sobbed. A feeling of infinite pity flooded the old man's heart. He, who despite the misery of his existence had never wept, saw that proud rich Martina was more miserable than a beggar.

168

'I'll do what I can,' he said. 'Go and calm yourself. Go now, because it's time for him to come home.'

She got up, wrapped herself well in the woollen cloth she had over her head when she arrived, and after the old man had looked out to make sure no one was watching, she went off slowly.

The night was chilly. The wind blew more strongly, ripping the first dead leaves from the trees. Not knowing why, Martina felt sadder and more desolate than ever. It seemed to her that the cold autumn wind pierced her right to her soul. As she passed by a cottage more wretched than the rest she raised her head and then lowered it at once, afraid lest an invisible being might divulge the grim idea that went through her. In that cottage there lived a man, a poor peasant, who had once asked her to lend him money.

'Lend!' she had replied ironically. 'And how can you pay it back?'

'If I cannot repay it,' he had replied, 'I will show you my gratitude in some other way. You can ask anything of me.'

She had understood. Just to get some money the man had put himself at her disposal even to the extent of committing a crime if need be. She hadn't needed anything then, and she had sent the man away. Now, passing by the ruined cottage, in the dark of the windy evening, she saw once again the peasant's ravaged, resolute face. She saw the misery burned into his eyes, his lips pale with hunger, his rough, dirty hands, still ready to do anything to drag some sort of goodness out of fate. The hate that gripped her selfish heart put a fearful idea into her mind. Like a portent of horror she passed by the poor man's cottage wrapped in her shawl, almost carried along by the wind.

That evening Isidoro had a long conversation with Costantino, begging him to avoid the tragedy that hung over all their heads. Costantino stared at the old man and smiled his bitter, mocking smile.

'What can happen?' he said. 'You yourself confirm that the old hag will say nothing to her son. Is Giovanna my wife or isn't she? If I go to her, it's because I have the right.'

169

'Oh, Son of God!' sighed Isidoro, clasping his hands together and shaking his head. 'You will destroy yourself. Look out. Watch out. Martina Dejas is capable of anything.'

Costantino's eyes shone with hatred. 'Listen,' he said, 'my heart is like a jug full of poison. One more drop will be enough to make it overflow. Woe to them who have made me do evil.'

So saying, he went out and wandered slowly through the gloomy night. He seemed to be lost in a wilderness of wind and loneliness. At about midnight he found himself almost without wanting it, like the first time, under Giovanna's window. Two roofs, one slightly higher than the other, allowed him to climb up and reach the window easily. He knocked and Giovanna opened it.

Martina, who was not asleep, realized that Giovanna and Costantino were spending the night together. 'Isidoro must have told Costantino what I said, and, far from moving him to pity, it has prompted him to take advantage of my weakness. Costantino must have decided that since I haven't had the courage to make my son unhappy by revealing the truth to him he might as well take advantage of me and come to see his mistress. He doesn't realize I'll do anything to save my son. It's between us two now, Costantino Ledda.'

One night, as he climbed down from Giovanna's window, the young man felt something cold graze his side, and in the darkness he glimpsed a black figure, a man with his head wrapped in a dark cloak.

Costantino hurled himself at the assassin's throat, and after a grim, silent struggle managed to throw the man to the ground and disarm him. Then he picked up the knife and took it, without even trying to find out who the man was. What did it matter to him who the killer was? It was the old woman's hand that wielded the knife.

Costantino himself tended the gash the knife had given him, and, like a hurt beast, he retired to lick his wounds in the old fisherman's hovel, for Isidoro was away from the village. For three days and three nights the young man lay on a mattress, sunk in dismal thoughts.

It was becoming cold. Outside the wind blew through the

hedges and the undergrowth and penetrated into the hovel, rippling the cobwebs and shaking the dust from the ceiling. From the tiny window, Costantino could see dark purple clouds sailing across the chill clarity of the sky, and he wanted to die. What else was there for him? He no longer loved Giovanna. He had taken her back out of obstinacy and frustration rather than desire, but he did not love her, because she had betrayed him in the days of his sorrow. Now he continued his love-affair with her out of hatred of the Dejas family. The thought that his death would bring joy to Martina was enough to revive him and kindle the blood in his veins.

He examined the dagger with which the unknown murderer had tried to kill him. It was an old Spanish knife with little spots of rust here and there like small clouds in a metallic sky. Someone, perhaps Martina herself, had rubbed the blade with ashes and ground it on a stone to make it serviceable again. As he looked at the knife, Costantino's eyes reddened with anger.

'They've taken everything away from me, and now they want to take my life. But I'll kill them. I remember once hearing a trial where the accused man had killed in self-defence and he was acquitted. They'll acquit me too if I defend myself. And if they don't acquit me . . .' He remembered his fellow convicts. The puffy yellow face of the King of Spades smiled lugubriously at the dismal end of the prison yard. At least they were in some ways my friends! Costantino thought. They were killers, but they made no attempt on my life.

On the third day that Costantino had been shut up in Isidoro's hovel, a driving rain began. Gloom shrouded the dreary little house, and black clouds massed outside the tiny square of the window. Drops of water began to leak through the roof. One in particular, large, cold, and unceasing, fell in the middle of the unlit hearth, beside the young man. He did not move, but when he saw the hearth was almost flooded he stretched out one arm and placed under the drips a saucepan that Isidoro used to cook the food in. The regular dismal drip, drip, drip was like the ticking of a clock. Night fell, cold and desolate. The rain went on pelting down. Costantino did not move. He had no wood to light the fire. He did not want to think about moving, going out, living. Held up perhaps by the rain in some neighbouring village, Isidoro did not return.

During the night Costantino became feverish. Dreams, memories, sadness and bitterness boiled in his confused mind. How long he continued in this state he could not have said. He remembered only the pelting noise of the rain, the wind that blew through the hovel, the water that dripped into the saucepan. From time to time he awoke from a feverish drowse, feeling a surge of exasperation and anguish as at one time he used to feel in prison when he awoke after a torrid night. Now a fierce desire sped through his blood. He wanted to take revenge on someone – to mutilate, to kill.

Another day passed, another night. The rain became still heavier. The drops of water fell inexorably until the saucepan filled up and overflowed. Hunger and fever were wasting the sick man. One night, he dreamed that a mad dog bit him in the stomach. He awoke shivering, thinking crazily that he had got rabies.

Towards evening the rain slackened off, but still did not stop. Someone knocked on the door and, thinking it was Isidoro, Costantino got up and opened it.

It was Giovanna. She was drenched and spattered with mud, her face was hidden by the border of the skirt that she had wrapped round her head. Costantino did not recognize her until she spoke.

'It's pitch dark in here,' she said. 'Are you there, Costantino?'

'What do you want?' he asked. 'Why have you come?'

'They told me the day before yesterday that you hadn't been to the shop for two days. The other night I realized you'd been attacked by someone. When they told me that you hadn't been seen I was terrified. I thought you had been killed. How I suffered for those two days. Hell could not be worse. Tonight I couldn't keep away any longer, so I came here. My mother is ill, my mother-in-law thinks I'm with her. Oh Holy Mary, Mother of God, dear Lord, hear how my heart beats. Costantino, I think I'm dying. I've run and run, I'm completely drenched. Won't you speak to me, Costantino?'

She stopped, anxious, terrified at what she had done,

shivering with cold and fear. Costantino did not reply. For a moment, in the darkness of the hovel, the only sounds to be heard were their breathing and the regular drip of the water as it fell into the saucepan.

'Why are you in the dark?' asked Giovanna. 'Why don't you speak? Are you ill? Are you hurt?'

'I'm ill. I've a slight fever,' he replied 'I haven't eaten for three days.'

'Where's Isidoro?'

'I don't know. He's travelling. He went to sell his ropes, and he hasn't got back yet. He'll come back soon. What's the matter with your mother?'

'A pain in the side, like Giacobbe Dejas, do you remember? But you, *you*?'

'I hope she dies!' cried Costantino, angry and sharp.

'Costantino!' reproved Giovanna.

'Yes,' he went on, 'I hope she dies, like I'm dying, here alone, kicked out like a dog, without help, without food, without warmth. I hope you all die, all of you who have killed me.'

He began to sob like a child and Giovanna felt a helpless, an agonizing pity. She tried to put her arms round his neck to comfort him, to cuddle up to him and seek refuge in him, in the dark cold that enclosed them outside and inside, but he pushed her away, stopped sobbing, and said harshly, 'Go away. Go away, now. I can't answer for what I do. I see I have become like a mad dog. I dreamed that a mad dog had bitten me. Go away. I'm going to vent my despair on someone soon. Go away!'

He pushed her, and she stared round frantically in the dark, confused, desperate, as she had not felt since the day of Costantino's conviction. He opened the door that she had left slightly ajar. It was still raining, but the wind had dropped and in the west the clouds were parting. The distant moon appeared through a tear in the clouds, making the rainy night still sadder and more tragic. Through that muddy light and the heavy curtain of rain, Costantino and Giovanna caught sight of a black figure moving away in the distance. Costantino did not recognize it, but Giovanna's heart skipped a beat.

'It's her, my mother-in-law. She followed me. She's spying on me,' said the young woman. 'I'm afraid, afraid.'

She shrank back in terror, not seeing what happened next. Costantino searching for something in the hovel. Then he rushed out into the funereal veil of rain, head down like a maddened bull. A piercing scream rent the night.

Never once during the rest of her unhappy life did Giovanna forget that scream. High and shrill, like the shriek of a wounded owl, it tore through her soul every time the ghost of murdered Martina returned to haunt her – or the ghost of Costantino in his living death in the tomb of forced labour, or the ghost of the drunkard Brontu Dejas, more dead and more wretched even than the murderer.

QUARTET ENCOUNTER

The purpose of this new paperback series is to bring together influential and outstanding works of twentieth-century European literature in translation. Each title has an introduction by a distinguished contemporary writer, describing a personal or cultural 'encounter' with the text, as well as placing it within its literary and historical perspective.

Quartet Encounter will concentrate on fiction, although the overall emphasis is upon works of enduring literary merit, whether biography, travel, history or politics. The series will also preserve a balance between new and older works, between new translations and reprints of notable existing translations. Quartet Encounter provides a much-needed forum for prose translation, and makes accessible to a wide readership some of the more unjustly neglected classics of modern European literature.

ENCOUNTER

Aharon Appelfeld · *The Retreat*

Translated from the Hebrew by Dalya Bilu,
with an introduction by Gabriel Josipovici
'A small masterpiece ... the vision of a remarkable poet'
New York Times Book Review

Grazia Deledda · *After the Divorce*

Translated from the Italian by Susan Ashe,
with an introduction by Sheila MacLeod
'What [Deledda] does is create the passionate complex
of a primitive populace' D.H. Lawrence

Carlo Emilio Gadda · *That Awful Mess on Via Merulana*

Translated from the Italian by William Weaver,
with an introduction by Italo Calvino
'One of the greatest and most original Italian novels
of our time' Alberto Moravia

Gustav Janouch · *Conversations with Kafka*

Translated from the German by Goronwy Rees,
with an introduction by Hugh Haughton
'I read it and was stunned by the wealth of new material ...
which plainly and unmistakably bore the stamp of Kafka's
genius' Max Brod

Henry de Montherlant · *The Bachelors*

Translated from the French and with an introduction
by Terence Kilmartin
'One of those carefully framed, precise and acid
studies on a small canvas in which French writers
again and again excel' V.S. Pritchett

Stanislaw Ignacy Witkiewicz · *Insatiability*

Translated from the Polish by Louis Iribarne,
with an introduction by Czeslaw Milosz
'A study of decay: mad, dissonant music; erotic perversion;
... and complex psychopathic personalities'
Czeslaw Milosz

DATE DUE